If you've ever chafed beneath the conclusion that you are only a woman, get ready to be set free to celebrate God's phenomenal call on your life and the giftings that are uniquely yours.

MICHELLE MCKINNEY HAMMOND, AUTHOR OF
IF MEN ARE LIKE BUSES, THEN HOW DO I CATCH ONE?

Only a Woman takes the reader on a fascinating journey where the final destination is spiritual growth and maturity. In her chapter of Overcoming the Pitfalls, Terri McFaddin writes: "God can turn a dark pitfall into a life-giving womb, where new character is formed and new visions are birthed." This book is a spiritual banquet, uniquely prepared by the author.

P. B. WILSON, AUTHOR OF
KNIGHT IN SHINING ARMOR—LIBERATED THROUGH SUBMISSION AND
SEVEN SECRETS WOMEN WANT TO KNOW

If you are a woman seeking to become all God has called you to be, you need to read *Only a Woman*. It will empower you to become the woman God intended you to be in your personal life, family life, church, and professional life.

DR. TONY EVANS, PRESIDENT, THE URBAN ALTERNATIVE SENIOR PASTOR,
OAK CLIFF BIBLE FELLOWSHIP

ONLY A WOMAN
CLAIMING YOUR AMAZING POWER IN CHRIST

TERRI McFADDIN

Multnomah® Publishers *Sisters, Oregon*

ONLY A WOMAN
published by Multnomah Publishers, Inc.

© 2001 by Terri McFaddin
International Standard Book Number: 1-57673-782-9

Cover image by Tony Stone Images

Scripture quotations are from:
The Holy Bible, New King James Version
© 1984 by Thomas Nelson, Inc.

Other translations cited:
The Holy Bible, New International Version (NIV) © 1973, 1984 by International
Bible Society, used by permission of Zondervan Publishing House
New American Standard Bible® (NASB) © 1960, 1977, 1995
by the Lockman Foundation. Used by permission.
Holy Bible, New Living Translation (NLT) © 1996. Used by permission of
Tyndale House Publishers, Inc. All rights reserved.
The Holy Bible, King James Version (KJV)

Multnomah is a trademark of Multnomah Publishers, Inc., and
is registered in the U.S. Patent and Trademark Office.
The colophon is a trademark of Multnomah Publishers, Inc.

Printed in the United States of America

For information:
MULTNOMAH PUBLISHERS, INC.•POST OFFICE BOX 1720•SISTERS, OREGON 97759

Library of Congress Cataloging-in-Publication Data:
McFaddin, Terri.
    Only a woman : claiming your amazing power in Christ / by Terri McFaddin.
        p.cm.   ISBN 1-57673-782-9 (pbk.)   1. Christian women–Religious life.
    I. Title. BV4527 .M392 2001   248.8'43–dc21   00-013152

04 05—10 9 8 7 6 5 4 3 2

To:

Jesus, the Author and Finisher of my faith

Pastor E. V. Hill
I thank God for allowing me to know and love one of the
greatest communicators of the gospel of Jesus Christ.
You are an awesome teacher and role model.

My daughters:

Roslyn McFaddin Ballard and
Theresa Adam McFaddin
My two greatest blessings in this world.

Contents

Acknowledgments

My family:

Roslyn, Rick, Theresa, Adam, Ashley, Anthony, Dad, Todd, Gary, Lillian, Jenni, Marlene, David, Aaron, Noni, Charles, Deborah, and the magnificent five.

Michelle McKinney Hammond:

Thank you for your encouragement and your introduction to Multnomah.

Bill Jensen:

Thank you for the free lunch. (smile)

Janet Bailey:

A faithful sister in Christ. Thanks to you and Trinity for hosting the Focus Group each week.

Nichole Palmer:

Thank you for making me a better writer. I also thank you for your editorial assistance.

Jeff Gerke:

A great editor. Thanks for rescuing me and for the yellow flowers.

Frank and Bunny Wilson:

Like a rock…thank you for always being there.

Marylyn McCoo and Billy Davis

Thank you for your love and spport.

Teresa Hairston—<u>Gospel Today</u> magazine

I owe you, lady.

Attorney Mark Little

You are an angel masquerading as a lawyer.

Jalilla Larseul, JL Media:

A faithful sister in Christ and a great publiscist.

The Study Guide Committee:

Nicole Palmer, Judi Jenkins, Janet Bailey, and Sandra Chapman. Thanks for your help and creativity.

The Focus Group Bible Study:

Dena, Rose, Katrina, Letha, Patrice, Yolanda, Sandra, Peggy, Phembia, Janet, Nicole, Judi, Angela, and all the other countless visitors to our Bible study. Thank you so much.

Bishop Kenneth and Tagotta Ulmer; the pastoral staff and the Faithful Central Bible Church family:

Thank you, Bishop, for your excellence and for challenging me to do great things for God.

Encouragers:

Vernon (my brother in Christ) and Pat Ashley—girlfirend! Colette Gumby—you are fierce! James and DeEtta West—write now! Andrew and Wanda Turner—godly and gracious. Paul Goodnight—the art of friendship. Juanita Scott—forever friends. Ed and Saundra Montgomery—a blessing. Florence LaRue—keep growing. Andrew and Vivica Merritt—hearts of gold. Jonathan and Burnell Slocum— keep laughing. Daynene Washington, Harry Young—faithful friends. Ollie Brown, Marilyn Beaubien, Paul Jackson and The Christian Entertainers Fellowship—keep winning souls. J. California Cooper— master storyteller. Michael Bennett, Debbie DuCre, Peggy Matthews— guardian angels. Velma Union (Ph.D. in love) and the professors and students at Fuller Theological Seminary. Whoever I am forgetting to thank—I love you!

Foreword

BY MICHELLE MCKINNEY HAMMOND

Many years ago I met a woman named Terri McFaddin. I recall the day vividly because it revolutionized the way I look at Scripture. There she was with her Bible, a collection of commentaries, dictionaries, and other study paraphernalia surrounding her. Though her tone was quiet, there was an intensity to her voice as she shared the revelations that had unfolded as she studied a passage in the book of Acts. As a baby Christian, I was completely mesmerized by her explanation. I purposed that day that when I grew up in the Lord, I wanted to be like her.

So now that you know that I am hopelessly prejudiced, let me tell you that you are in for a treat—no, a life-changing experience—as you read this book.

Some may look at Terri and, judging by surface assumptions, conclude that she is only a woman. Nothing could be further from the truth. She is a powerful vessel, an example of what God can do with a yielded servant.

Trust me: As you read this book, you will see yourself. Your questions, your hopes, your struggles, and yes, even your failures. But you will also see the victory that can be yours as you embrace the principles Terri shares. If you've ever chafed beneath the conclusion that you are only a woman, get ready to be set free to celebrate God's phenomenal call on your life and the giftings that are uniquely yours.

I am so excited that you are getting ready to discover what I have known for some time: Terri has a word for women that needs to be heard. Not only is she a master storyteller, rightly dividing the Word into profound insights that are sure to bless you, she is honest, real, and compassionate in her correction.

So read and be changed. Digest the words and be empowered to be all that you were created to be—a force to be reckoned with according to the power of God at work within you.

PART ONE

THE STORY OF A WOMAN

ut I am only a woman." She wept as she spoke these words to her husband, who lay cradled in her arms. The village was under attack by a rebel army. Her husband was a brave leader, but in the midst of protecting his family and his village, he had been gravely wounded.

"You must make your way to the neighboring village and ask them for help," he whispered to her.

Trembling with fear, she tried to answer. "But how can I make a journey through enemy territory? What about the baby? Besides, I don't know how to fight. I'm only a woman."

Her wounded husband reached up, touched her face, and whispered, "God is with you." Then his body went limp in her arms.

The woman lifted her voice and wept out loud. "Please don't leave me! I love you. How can I live without you?" Her heart pounded like the fist of a woman who had been buried alive in a tomb. Fear gripped her, making it almost impossible to breathe. She closed her eyes tightly, trying to make sense of what was happening. Perhaps she had fainted; maybe she was dreaming.

She saw herself running through the corridors of her mind, locking the doors of reality, retreating to a quiet place, where she found a pleasant memory: Her husband touching her face for the very first time. The woman smiled as she drifted back to days gone by...

Back then, she had just blossomed into womanhood and was plagued with a secret fear that she would never be married. One by one her friends found husbands, but there was something peculiar about her view of life that made it difficult for most of the men in her village to feel comfortable with her. Of course she became even more anxious as, one by one, the young women around her became aglow with the joy of carrying children. The woman's prayers for a husband could be heard in every part of the heavenlies.

Finally the Lord sent a perfect man. They fit into each other's lives like two interlocking pieces of a puzzle. They married on a warm spring day, on a hillside just at the foot of a crystal blue waterfall. "I will love you as I love my own flesh," her new husband said. "I will protect you and even lay down my life for you." Then he gently touched her face and kissed her forehead. The covenant was sealed and they began their lives together.

They lived in a small house that was empty of material possessions but was filled with love. Their first child joined them at the end of the first year of their marriage. The woman walked quietly among her neighbors, carrying her new son and beaming with pride as they fussed over her beautiful baby.

"Look how strong he is—just like his father!" said an old woman, smiling.

"You are a blessed woman to have a good husband and such a fine son," another woman remarked.

Each day, after taking her daily walk through the village and being refreshed by a shower of compliments, she would return to her house to care for her husband and to enjoy her quiet, peaceful life.

Suddenly the memory evaporated and the screams of her people jarred her back to the moment. The woman looked around at the disheveled room, then at the lifeless body of her husband. She didn't know what to do, but desperation forced her to think and to reach a decision. She would search out one of the soldiers and give him her husband's orders. Surely a brave young man could find a way to penetrate the enemy lines and reach their allies in the next village.

Holding her child tightly in her arms, the woman covered her husband's body with a cloth and left her house. She kept to the shadows as she searched the ravaged village for a soldier. After a long while she came upon a young man who recognized her face. "My husband is dead," she explained. "Our village is now without a leader. One of the soldiers must go to the neighboring village for help."

The young man gave the woman a regretful look. "Only a handful of soldiers are left to fight. If I leave now, everyone will be killed. You must do it yourself."

"How can I?" she protested. "Can't you see that I'm only a woman? How am I supposed to take my baby across enemy lines?"

"I don't know," the soldier said. "I only know that I can't help you." He shook his head and walked away.

The woman reeled from his rejection. How foolish and naive she had been for thinking of her little world as a perfect place where she would never have to live without the help of a man. The woman held her child close to her breast and went back to what was left of her house. She sat on the floor and began to weep and pray. *Lord, I don't have the strength of a man and I don't know what to do. Lord, please help me.*

The sound of fighting and the smell of burning houses filled the night air. The woman's hands trembled as she filled a sack with food and a jug with water. She tied her child tightly to her back with a piece of cloth. Under the cover of night she made her way into the forest, headed in the direction of the neighboring village.

All around her she could hear the voices of enemy soldiers, but something calmed her heart as she made her way through the woods. She hid herself in thickets, down in riverbeds, and once in the hollow of a tree trunk. Perhaps it was because she had already looked into the eyes of death that she was no longer intimidated by its presence.

Once a group of enemy soldiers came so close to her hiding place that she could hear them breathing. It was then that she knew for certain God had taken away her fear and was covering her with His hand, making her invisible to human eyes. As she continued her journey, she began to listen for the voice of the Lord in her heart, telling her when to move and when to be still. When her child began to fret she sat down in the darkness, fed him from her breast, then rocked him gently until he was quiet.

As the gray mist of dawn filled the sky, the woman's heart began beating fast—she had finally reached the other side of the forest. Now she was just a short distance from the meadow filled with tall grass that would hide her as she crept over the hill to the village. As she darted between the tall trees, she felt beneath her feet loose dirt, wet leaves, small rocks—and then suddenly, nothing.

Down she plunged, trying to stifle the scream that rose to her throat. When she hit bottom, she realized with horror that she had fallen into a deep, dark pit—a trap set by the enemy.

The shooting pain in her legs forced groans from her mouth. *Thank God, my baby is unhurt,* she realized with relief. Fear gripped her anew as she heard footsteps approaching the pit. A soldier had heard her moaning. His figure was silhouetted against the night sky; she watched as he raised his weapon to execute her. Suddenly the frightened baby cried out. The soldier dropped his weapon and knelt by the pit. "Who's there?"

"Please help me," the woman said in a trembling voice.

The soldier found a rope and climbed into the pit to rescue the woman and her child. Once they were both safe, they heard the voice of his commanding officer in the distance. "Did you kill the prisoner?"

The man looked at the frightened woman and child, then turned in the direction of the voice. "No!" he called back. "It was only a woman."

Before the soldier could question her further, the woman fell on her face and began to weep. She looked up at him gratefully. "Thank you, kind sir, for showing mercy to me and my child," she said. "I beg of you to tell me your name that I may keep it in my heart forever. When my son comes of age, I will tell him about the brave soldier that saved our lives."

The soldier seemed unable to speak. Finally he told her his name, then asked the question that would mean life or death to the woman and her child: "Where were you going?"

The soldier's question struck terror in the woman's heart. She prayed to the Lord and tried to calm herself. She could hear words spilling from her lips: "I am going to visit friends in a nearby village."

The silence seemed eternal as the soldier thought about her answer. Finally he drew a deep breath and said, "Do you have food and water?"

The woman could hardly believe her ears. "I—I must have dropped my supplies when I fell into the pit," she faltered.

The soldier helped the woman to her feet, supplied her with bread and water, and sent her on her way. Before disappearing into the forest, the woman tore a piece of red fabric from the hem of her dress and held it out to the soldier.

"If you tie this around your arm, it will protect you and bring you a blessing," she told him.

The soldier seemed reluctant, but he took the fabric and wrapped it around his arm. He assured her that if she stayed on the path she would not have to worry about falling into another pit.

The woman bowed, thanked him again, and left.

She reached the neighboring village by midafternoon, and there she told her story to the elders, pleading with them to return with her and help save her village.

The council of wise men gave her petition much thought. Finally the leader spoke: "Tell us why we should risk the lives of our soldiers by coming to the aid of your village."

The woman was not prepared for such a question. She thought of her people, suffering and dying, as these men asked questions. But in this desperate hour the woman found the words: "I vow this day that if your enemies ever rise up against you, my people will become your people; when our sons grow up, they will become soldiers who will come to your defense."

The elders did not answer the woman but instead walked a short distance away; for a long while they discussed the matter amongst themselves. Then the leader picked up a horn and sounded the alarm. Soldiers immediately gathered. After receiving their orders, they prepared to go to the woman's village to drive out the enemy.

"There is one other favor I must ask of you," the woman said to the elders. "If you see a soldier with a red band tied around his arm, please spare his life. He saved the lives of me and my child." The elders agreed.

On that very day they drove the enemy from her village and saved her people. When the fighting had ended, the people honored the woman with a great celebration. They sang her praises, saying that God had performed a miracle using her weakness to crush a strong enemy. Over and over they sang:

> She rocked her child with gentle hands.
> Then fearlessly she took command.
> She cared not if she lived or died,
> As long as God was glorified.

The songs of thanksgiving to God continued to fill the air even as they buried their dead and removed the carnage of battle from the streets. The woman felt only partly alive as she watched her husband's body being lowered into the ground. Time seemed to stand still as the celebration ended and she settled in to what was left of her ruined house. She could never return to the past, and she couldn't imagine facing the future alone.

The people in the village continued to treat the woman as a heroine, but she was numb to everything around her. One day as she was out walking, a group of young men crossed her path. Among them was the young soldier that had refused her plea to go to the neighboring village for help.

He approached the woman respectfully. "I want to apologize for not honoring your request on the night you asked me to go for help," he said, bowing his head.

The woman smiled. "Perhaps it was not God's will for you to go. You might have been killed."

One of the other young men could no longer contain himself. "Forgive my curiosity, but none of us know how you managed to cross enemy lines. After all, you were not a soldier—you are only a woman! How did you—?"

The young man was interrupted by the laughter of a very old man who sat beneath a nearby tree. He bowed his head in deep reverence to the woman, then spoke: "Young man, when you are older you will come to realize that there are some things in this life that 'only a woman' can do."

CHAPTER ONE

The Gateway to Change

ecoming a champion for God is a challenge. In order for a woman to make life-changing decisions, she must first come to a place of self-discovery. Without a sense of true identity and significance in the sight of God, it is almost impossible to stand apart from the parade of mindless bodies that allow themselves to be taken into captivity by enemy forces. In the story of the woman who saved her village, it is important to note the steps that led to her complete transformation and victory.

In the opening line of the story, the woman made a very revealing statement about herself. In the face of overwhelming crisis she cried out, "But I am only a woman." She was afraid. At that moment the only thing she could find to hide behind was her gender. If the truth were told, the best of us have at one time or another made excuses to avoid unpleasant tasks. Maybe you should ask yourself what kind of excuses you make to avoid facing problems.

A married woman may hope that her husband will rescue her from dilemma. When she discovers that her husband doesn't have the ability or interest to help her, she might blame him if the crisis turns out unfavorably.

A single woman might offer the excuse that she has failed at a particular task because she has no one in her life to provide the help and support she needs. She may even lament that if she was married she wouldn't have to face certain difficulties.

An older woman could put the blame on her advanced age for avoiding an unpleasant task, even as a younger woman might claim that she doesn't have the experience or maturity to deal with weighty matters.

The excuses for running away from crisis include lack of education, finances, and emotional support. The ultimate Christian excuse may be one that you've heard before: "The Lord told me not to get involved."

Don't feel bad. When you're gripped by fear, it's perfectly normal to look for an escape hatch. But in a real crisis, a great inner struggle will erupt between the person you believe you are and the person God has called you to become. I call it the war between the God-image and the self-image.

The God-image is the person God intended you to be from the womb—the person with specific gifts, purpose, and calling.

The self-image is the person you perceive yourself to be based on the influences of your environment and your culture.

The book of Judges gives a classic example of a woman who probably began her life with no idea of the power of her God-given image. Her name was Deborah, and as her relationship with the Lord began to unfold, she went from being an ordinary housewife to settling disputes as a judge and fighting for the deliverance of her people.

The Bible does not tell us much about Deborah's background, but we do know that she was married to a man named Lapidoth and that she lived a modest life in the hill country of Ephraim. It was her custom to sit beneath a palm tree, probably weaving baskets or maybe making clay jars to hold food and water for her family. As time passed, the palm tree on the hillside of Ephraim became the seat of government where Deborah prophesied and judged Israel.

Deborah may have been "only a woman," but she eventually became a prophetess, psalmist, judge, and mother of Israel. The name *Deborah* means "bee." Bumblebees are known to be industrious, producing sweetness—yet capable of stinging if provoked. When the enemies of Israel provoked this woman of God, she took on a new role: Deborah the warrior.

> Village life ceased, it ceased in Israel,
> Until I, Deborah, arose,
> Arose a mother in Israel. (Judges 5:7)

In our culture we certainly don't think of a mother as a brave champion, but Deborah used her nurturing skills for the glory of God. Like a dutiful mother, she persuaded the warrior Barak to fight against the enemies of Israel. When he refused to take up the challenge without Deborah by his side, once again Deborah went, like a caring mother, to face the Canaanite army.

Allowing your God-image to prevail infuses your daily work with power. For example, if part of your God-image is having a mother's heart, then you are one who is responsible for the well-being of the family. It may be your immediate family, your neighborhood family, or your national family. Somehow you always find yourself "mom" to your dormitory, your job, your church, or even to strangers at the mall that need advice about what shoes to buy or how to find parking level D. People are drawn to you for wise counsel and consistent care.

Judge Deborah also proved a strong role model to the women of her day. She presented an image of strength and fearlessness, compassion and commitment, all wrapped up in a mother's heart. She set a standard for other women and encourages us to do even greater works for the kingdom of God.

JAEL'S STORY

A young woman named Jael, the wife of Heber the Kenite, became worthy of Deborah's song of praise. The song of Deborah (Judges 5:24–31), tells how God arranged for gentle Jael to encounter Sisera, commander of the Canaanite army.

Sisera, who was fighting against Israel, came to the house of Jael and asked her to hide him from Barak and his soldiers. Jael graciously brought him into her house and gave him warm milk to drink and a place to rest his head. When Sisera was fast asleep, Jael proved a potent force against the enemies of Israel: She drove a stake through Sisera's head while he slept. The woman who took his life was "only" a woman—thoughtful enough to ensure he left this world with a well-rested body and a bellyful of warm milk.

I am certain that before Sisera arrived at Jael's house, she wasn't spending her time thinking of ways to assassinate a wicked man. As she swept the kitchen floor and straightened up her house, she might have laughed at the thought of a crisis that would transform her into a heroine that generations to come would remember. Yet when Sisera appeared at Jael's door, something rose up in her that probably surprised her and everyone else who heard the story.

Jael's story reminds us that when the pressure is on, whatever strength is in us will rise to the surface. If on the inside we are selfish or weak, then when faced with a challenge that is how we will respond. If we are truly courageous and giving, our actions will reflect this. When the circumstances of life show us what we are really made of, many times we are as surprised as everyone else.

Both Jael and Deborah acted in their God-image to perform the task He had ordained them to accomplish. They were made aware of their purpose: to glorify God. With the power of God at work within them, they achieved victory.

CHAMPIONS AND HEROES:
IS ONE BETTER THAN THE OTHER?

Before closing the story of Deborah and Jael, I want to pose a question: What is the difference between a champion and a hero?

A champion is a person that dedicates herself to serious training and preparation for the purpose of defending a right or winning a prize. A champion is always prepared and is determined to find victory: "I press toward the goal for the prize of the upward call of God in Christ Jesus" (Philippians 3:14).

A hero, on the other hand, is a person that may be untrained and unprepared but shows great courage in the face of crisis. A hero must have an unselfish heart. This is what allows her to be used by God at the risk of her own life. "Through God we will do valiantly / For it is He who shall tread down our enemies" (Psalm 60:12).

Please understand that in the face of adversity it is better to be a *champion* with a plan of action than a *hero* that randomly springs into action. Training makes you better prepared to fulfill the Lord's will—to act effectively and productively. A hero, while still an important player, may falter for lack of skill and preparation.

Frankly, this is why so many marriages and families are destroyed. Even if a woman is willing to give her life to save her family, she may fail due to a lack of training to do so.

It is not uncommon for heroic parents to conduct a desperate search for someone to help their child who is in trouble or out of control. If they don't find support, they stand helplessly by as the child is devoured by the enemy. But if they think like spiritual champions, then they will be fully prepared when enemies appear at their front door—or anywhere else in their lives.

In his book *Spiritually Fit to Run the Race,* Kenneth Ulmer says, "Many of you are losing spiritual battle after spiritual battle, not because you don't know Jesus, or because you doubt the promises of God, but because you're not spiritually fit."[1]

Deborah and Jael were both used mightily by the Lord, but Deborah did greater things for God because she was a champion—fully trained and fully prepared. Jael was a woman with a godly heart who became a hero for God when faced suddenly with an unexpected challenge.

By now you may be asking yourself, *How do I become a champion for God?* I am so glad you asked! The first thing you must do is to discover your God-image. Earlier I said that when it comes to facing a challenge, your self-image will lock horns in a life-and-death struggle with your God-image. The outcome of the crisis will determine which of these images will take authority over the other. I am praying that in the midst of crisis your God-image will prevail.

THE WAR BETWEEN SELF-IMAGE AND GOD-IMAGE

Why am I praying for your God-image to take complete control? Because self-image is based on feelings and perceptions that may have nothing to do with whom God intended you to be. With one blow to the ego from someone you admire, your self-image can be damaged. The self-image can be unpredictable because not one of us knows our real self until put to the test. Therefore you cannot depend on self as a source of assurance and confidence in the face of a crisis. Self-image may leave you questioning your own judgment and abilities. You will blame yourself for things over which you have no control and no power to change.

Self-image is also culture-based. Something as shallow as the latest "look" can shake your self-image—thin is "in" and you feel overweight; you think you're the wrong size, color, or age; you are being scorned by working women for choosing to be a stay-at-home mom; you feel left behind for choosing to pour yourself into your studies while your friends are out having a good time; the voice of insecurity whispers convincingly that you could lose your job because of your age, race, or gender.

The point is that if you allow the shallowness of self-image to rule, you will lack the confidence to pursue all that God has ordained for your life. You will be too intimidated to become a champion for the kingdom of God.

If, however, the God-image is allowed to rule, it will not be affected by the acceptance or rejection of popular trends. The Scriptures confirm that the God-image has the power to turn an ordinary woman into an effective weapon against the kingdom of darkness. They speak of "Him who is able to do exceedingly abundantly above all that we ask or think, according to the power that works in us" (Ephesians 3:20).

There is more supernatural power at work in us than we could ever imagine. Kingdoms and mighty warriors have been destroyed because all they could see was the seemingly weak exterior of a woman. Many have failed to understand that "God has chosen the weak things of the world to put to shame the things which are mighty" (1 Corinthians 1:27b).

The woman in the opening story represents the inner struggles that women go through as it relates to God-image versus self-image. Many women (even those that say otherwise) are not sure who they really are and what their full range of potential is. A crisis can bring everything to light.

> And suddenly, a woman who had a flow of blood for twelve
> years came from behind and touched the hem of His
> [Jesus'] garment. For she said to herself, "If only I may touch
> His garment, I shall be made well." (Matthew 9:20–21)

Think of the courage it took for this woman to break Jewish law and come into a public place with an "uncleanness" in her body.

By Jewish law, for her to touch Jesus (or any other person) was to defile Him with her uncleanness. Yet the Lord was not offended when the woman put her faith into action. Instead of rebuking her, He applauded her faith and healed her infirmity (v. 22).

This woman lived a life of shame and rejection for twelve years before finding the courage to escape her self-image. When she discovered her God-image, she was able to tap in to the "power that works in us." This power is available to all who connect with Jesus.

WHY WOMEN DEVALUE THEMSELVES

The absence of a God-image and the presence of a damaged self-image can cause a woman to devalue the powerful person God created her to be. For many, the roots of our poor self-esteem can be traced to the environment in which we live.

A woman may devalue herself because she has been devalued by people that shaped her thinking. She may be loved and cared for in a protective environment, but if that environment promotes control instead of growth, it will ultimately do more harm than good. Sometimes the most loving acts of care and protection prove to be subtle ways of telling a woman that she is not capable of caring for herself.

Without a strong God-image to draw on, a woman can become ensnared in patterns of negative behavior. The following exhibit a few of these behaviors:

Rebellious behavior. This can be demonstrated by secretive or overt rebellion. A woman who finds herself subject to oppressive authority can become rebellious as a way of demonstrating hurt and frustration. Rebellion can be a means of striking back at a controlling or critical authority figure. It can take on the form of wild, seductive behavior. The rebellious woman may accept any viewpoint that is in opposition to that of her controller. She may join radical movements or associate closely with people from alternative lifestyles. Bulimia, anorexia, and drug and alcohol abuse are common ways in which the rebellious woman expresses anger and vents frustration.

Passive-aggressive behavior. This form of rebellion is found in a woman who fails to live up to her oppressor's expectations. She is both consciously and subconsciously sabotaging the people trying to control her by refusing to take action. She speaks of going back to school or getting a better job, losing weight or decorating her home, but she never takes action. She makes promises that she does not keep. She is neglectful of important things that need to be accomplished. She makes excuses for everything. Behind her façade of incompetence lies a very capable woman, but she harbors a deep-seated anger that won't allow her to please those she resents the most.

Overly pleasing behavior. The pleaser is a woman that has fallen into the trap of trying to make everyone else happy. The pleaser will do anything for affirmation and acceptance from the person whose attention she craves. She has no apparent dreams, goals, or desires outside of doing the controller's bidding. It may be a parent, husband, boss, boyfriend, or even a child—any of them are capable of control.

Fear-filled behavior. For the fearful woman, the damage inflicted may not have been as gradual or as subtle. She has likely experienced sexual, physical, or emotional abuse, leaving her so fearful and insecure that she finds it difficult to take a risk in any area of her life. She is afraid to speak up for herself; she is afraid to speak up for others. She purposefully stifles her voice.

Tragically, all of these behaviors are self-perpetuating—they allow the self-image to remain the ruler, even as the God-image lies dormant.

THE BRIDGE FROM SELF-IMAGE TO GOD-IMAGE

The God-image can remain undiscovered as a woman's life ebbs away, or God can intervene. He knows how to disguise Himself, and sometimes in the form of a crisis He will slip into the life of a rebel, a passive-aggressive, a pleaser—or even an ordinary woman who is not aware of the power lying within her. The Lord will continue to work on a woman until maturity, purpose, and liberty are fully formed.

He did this in the life of the woman in our opening story. In a moment of crisis, God intervened and changed her from a powerless, fearful woman to a woman who earned the title "heroine" in her village.

Without a doubt, women have made many strides in the areas of social and economic equality. But there are still cultures around the world where the laws of the land, community, family, and/or religion view women as *beloved inferiors*. Jesus came to make women *beloved equals* in the eyes of man, just as they are in the eyes of God. He restored to women that which had been taken from them—their dignity and their value. The apostle Paul echoed the heart of Christ as he wrote,

> There is neither Jew nor Greek, there is neither slave nor free, there is neither male nor female; for you are all one in Christ Jesus. (Galatians 3:28)

If you are experiencing adversity in your family, job, or finances, perhaps the Lord is using these to move you from a limiting self-image to an expansive God-image. Please remember that as the Lord works to move you from a place of weakness to a place of strength, it is not only for your personal development; it is also to train you as a champion for His kingdom. God knows there are things that "only a woman" can accomplish in His service.

CHAPTER TWO

Waiting to Be Rescued

nce again, let's revisit our opening story of the woman in distress. Her declaration that she was "only a woman" fell on deaf ears as her husband lay dying in her arms. There will be times when the people we depend upon will fail to make real our hopes and dreams. Unemployment, misplaced priorities, and illness are but a few of the circumstances that can bring about disappointment in the people we depend upon the most.

This way of thinking is prevalent because fairy tales and movie myths have deceived women for centuries. The stories of Snow White and Cinderella are etched in the minds of women around the world. I have watched women sink deeper and deeper into fantasy, shame, poverty, and depression while waiting to be rescued. Deep in their hearts is a childlike belief that Prince Charming will gallop into her enchanted forest and find her, the beautiful maiden, sleeping soundly in the midst of her chaos. The fantasy cannot be complete without the fairy-tale wedding that will rescue her forever from the cares of this world.

But guess what? After years of marriage, some women are still waiting for their husband (Prince Charming) to remove his feet from the coffee table, turn off the football game, and save them from bill collectors, loneliness, parenting problems, and stopped-up plumbing.

It never occurs to these women that the men on the couch are not rescuing them because they don't know how to rescue themselves.

Most men are not looking for women who need to be rescued. Rather, they are looking for women that demonstrate a healthy level of spiritual and emotional maturity. If a man has to find a woman who needs to be rescued in order to validate his masculinity, then watch out—there's trouble ahead.

GOD HAS A BETTER PLAN

The woman in our story looked for someone to rescue her from her dilemma. She ran through the ravaged village looking for a big, strong man to help her. Surely when a soldier looked into her sorrowful eyes, he would be moved to bravely cross through enemy lines and save the day. But just like the woman's husband, the young soldier she encountered was powerless to help her. She was on her own.

God stands in the shadows watching as reality splashes cold water in the woman's face. She is forced to awaken from her fairy tale.

There are times when we attempt to use our feminine charms to lure someone into rescuing us from an adverse circumstance. But when the God who loves us and wants the very best for us decides that it is time for us to reach our full potential as women, our rescuers will tell us what the young soldier said to the woman: "You'll have to do it yourself!" Once again God smiles from the shadows.

After a painful rejection from her would-be rescuer, the woman in our opening story fell to her knees and prayed, *Lord, I'm only a woman. I don't have the strength of a man and I don't know what to do. Lord, please…help me.*

Let's take a big theological step together. I want to share with you an important concept about the word *help*. Let me begin with Genesis 2:18: "And the LORD God said, It is not good that the man should be alone; I will make him an help meet for him" (KJV). The term *help meet* or *helper* means much more than a woman acting out the role of a humble servant. In the New King James Version of the Bible you will find a more fitting definition of help meet: "...a helper comparable to him."

In the original language (Hebrew), the word for "help" is *ezer*.[1] The prophet Ezra's name is derived from the root of this word. Ezra means "the Lord has helped." There are two places in the Bible where a woman is referred to as an *ezer*—or helper—of a man. Both references are found in the second chapter of Genesis, verses 18 and 20. But countless Scriptures refer to God as the *ezer* of humankind. For example:

> The God of my father was my help [ezer]. (Exodus 18:4)
> Happy is he who has the God of Jacob for his help [ezer].
>   (Psalm 146:5a)
> O Israel, you are destroyed, but your help [ezer] is from Me.
>   (Hosea 13:9)

New Testament writers refer to the Holy Spirit as the *comforter* or *helper*: "And I will pray the Father, and He will give you another Helper, that He may abide with you forever" (John 14:16).

It is vital to understand that a biblical *ezer* is one that helps from a position of strength, not weakness. The Hebrew word that describes God as the helper of man is the same word used to describe woman as the helper of man. As God is the *ezer* of humankind, so women are *ezers* of men. Therefore God has armed women with a special strength to provide help when and where it is needed. The myth about the helplessness of a "damsel in distress" need not be true. A woman that discovers her God-image becomes the powerfully feminine *ezer*.

Understanding the strength of a woman can raise many questions. We read in the New Testament: "Husbands, likewise, dwell with them with understanding, giving honor to the wife, as to the weaker vessel" (1 Peter 3:7). Please note that Peter did not call the wife the "weak" vessel, which would have suggested that the husband is "strong." Rather, the apostle said the wife should be honored as the *weaker* vessel. This would suggest that both men and women have weaknesses. Peter then called the husband to honor his wife in the areas where she is weaker than him. For example, women do not have the natural physical strength of men. If a woman is pregnant or elderly, she can be extremely vulnerable.

At no point does this Scripture suggest that women do not have areas of great strength. God has created a delicate balance of inter-dependence between men and women. In the areas where men are strong, women may be weaker. In the areas where women are strong, men may be weaker.

USING YOUR POWER WITHOUT OVERPOWERING

The challenge for most women is to know how to use their strength as helpers without emasculating, overpowering, or belittling men. The dying warrior in our opening story needed his wife to embark on a dangerous mission in order to save their village. Under normal cir-cumstances he would never have called on her to attempt such a feat, but when he needed a strong helper, he looked to the woman as his rescuer. In turn, the woman looked to her heavenly Father, the great *Ezer,* to become her rescuer as well as the true rescuer of her village.

It is not unusual for a woman to suddenly find herself acting as a rescuer in times of trouble. The strongest of husbands can fall ill or encounter financial difficulty. Even when there is no major crisis, there are areas in which a woman is more skilled than the man in her life. She may be a better mechanic or better at handling legal matters. A dear friend once told me, "It's not what a woman brings to the table, it's how she presents her gift." The greatest challenge for the female *ezer* is to not abuse her power to help, causing her husband to become weak and dependent rather than a strong covering over his family.

A woman's poor self-image and the absence of her God-image

can also fuel an unhealthy need for control. In these cases she looks for someone who needs her help on a continual basis, then complains about being trapped in hopeless situations.

Then there are women who are neither interested in being in control nor plagued by insecurity. They simply do not understand the art and the boundaries of being the helper. The Bible gives very clear directives that show how a woman can be an effective helper. Here's one:

> Wives, likewise, be submissive to your own husbands, that even if some do not obey the word, they, without a word, may be won by the conduct of their wives, when they observe your chaste conduct accompanied by fear. (1 Peter 3:1–2)

A wonderful story is hidden within this seemingly innocent passage. Where Peter appears simply to be encouraging women in the areas of submission, good conduct, and reverence toward their husbands, there is much more to it.

In the early church, many women embraced the Christian faith without their husbands' permission. The elders of the church did not want this to cause upheaval in their homes, so they gave the women some wise counsel. They believed that an increase in the wives' godly behavior and a deeper reverence for their husbands would cause the unbelieving spouses to seek out the source of their wives' transformations. What Peter recommended was not submission because the women were weak, but rather submission because it was the key to their husbands' salvation.[2]

EXAMPLE OF AN *EZER*

Contemporary women need to see a thriving example of the *ezer* in action so as to have a godly model to follow. God has provided direction for this in His Word:

> The older women likewise, that they be reverent in behavior, not slanderers, not given to much wine, teachers of good things—that they admonish the young women to love their husbands, to love their children, to be discreet, chaste, homemakers, good, obedient to their own husbands, that the word of God may not be blasphemed. (Titus 2:3–5)

I strongly recommend that younger women desiring to become effective as helpers spend time with older women that have years of experience as wives, mothers, and women of God. An effective *ezer* knows how to encourage her mate. She knows the proper time and place to give suggestions, not orders. She knows how to effectively pray so that blessings are showered down upon her family. Most of all, she is a *giver* as well as a *forgiver.* While she enjoys the times of happiness that her husband brings to her life, he is not the entire source of her joy. The joy of the Lord is her strength—and it is this power that makes her an irreplaceable *ezer* in her home.

God also has an awesome plan for the unmarried woman to play an important role as the *ezer*/helper.

> There is a difference between a wife and a virgin. The unmarried woman cares about the things of the Lord, that she may be holy both in body and in spirit. But she who is married cares about the things of the world—how she may please her husband. (1 Corinthians 7:34)

The unmarried woman who walks in her God-image is of great value to the Lord as His maidservant and helper. The Bible is filled with examples of unmarried women who were some of God's greatest servants. As followers of Jesus, they broke religious and social traditions by traveling with Him and working alongside His male disciples. One of the most prominent women who served the Lord was Mary Magdalene, a woman who was delivered from seven demons (Luke 8:2). When she first encountered Jesus, she was a woman trapped in a terrible crisis. Once she was healed, she dedicated her life to the Savior.

There were also the two sisters of Lazarus, Mary and Martha, who ministered to Jesus. Even after the death and resurrection of Jesus, several single women helped to establish the New Testament church. One of them was Lydia, who was a successful businesswoman and probably unmarried. She was among the women who sought the Lord and gladly opened her home to Paul and Silas.

Unmarried woman, never feel that you have less to offer the Lord as single *ezers*. As our world becomes engulfed in the chaos of sin, the Lord is pouring out His Spirit on the *ezers*. For the unmarried woman, the sky is the limit when it comes to serving the Lord. There is no husband to keep you from getting involved in fighting for the lives of unborn babies, ministering to young people and the elderly, developing economic ventures, and building strong ministries on domestic and foreign mission fields. God is anointing single women as the unhindered helpers who carry out His will.

EXTRAORDINARY *EZERS*, PAST AND PRESENT

I hope you understand that women as *ezers*—those women who refuse to wait on a rescuer—do much more than help husbands. Our history is filled with brave women whom God raised up to be the *ezers* to a wide spectrum of people in need. Like the woman in our opening story, these women became *ezers* as a result of crises.

Cindy Lightner and a small band of women were outraged after a teenage girl was killed by a drunk driver that was a repeat offender. In their fight to keep this driver from getting behind the wheel again, they organized Mothers Against Drunk Drivers (MADD). Because of their *help,* laws have been passed to protect people from drunk drivers.[3]

Sixty-three-year-old Clara Hale had been a foster mother for most of her adult life. In 1975, when babies born addicted to drugs and infected with AIDS were being abandoned, she opened her small New York apartment to care for them. Before her death in 1993 she had founded the Hale House and cared for more than 500 AIDS and drug-addicted babies. Her daughter, Dr. Lorraine Hale, continues the work her mother began.[4]

Florence Nightingale was born in England to a family of wealth and privilege. Her family was outraged when she felt called to enter the Protestant Deaconesses program in Paris, where she trained to care for the sick. In 1850, when England and France went to war with Russia, England's Secretary of War called on Florence for *help*. Along with thirty-three other women whom she trained personally, Florence went to the battlefield in Crimea. When the war ended, she established the first school to train nurses.[5]

Harriet "Moses" Tubman was an ex-slave that *helped* more than 300 slaves escape to North America and Canada. She was known as the leading conductor of the Underground Railroad. In fact, in 1849 a reward of forty thousand dollars was offered for Harriet's capture. During the Civil War she *helped* the Union Army by working as a nurse and a spy.[6]

Beneath Mother Teresa's fragile exterior was the powerful spirit of the *ezer.* You may never become a missionary and care for the people of Calcutta as she did, but you can still be the *ezer* she was. Mother Teresa wrote this: "The greatest fulfillment is doing God's will. We do not have to do great things, only small things with great love."[7]

None of these women, including the woman in our opening story, planned to become rescuers of their people. Each of them simply answered the call that God has put forth to every woman: *Come, be my ezer. I have plans that only you, a woman, can fulfill.*

CHAPTER THREE

Accepting the Challenge

The woman in our opening story was probably numb from head to toe as she strapped her child to her back and started out through the forest. She moved forward, following God's invisible hand. He whispered words that only she could hear: *Keep moving, don't stop. Rest in this place. I'll supply your needs. Don't be afraid. I won't let them hurt you.* Many times during her journey she was so close to danger that she could feel the enemy's breath on her skin. But God continued to lead her as she walked through the valley of the shadow of death.

KNOWING GOD'S VOICE

One of the most important keys to our survival as women living in a world filled with crisis is listening for the still, small voice of God. People ask me all the time, "How do I know if God is speaking to me?" That's a very good question. A few important rules may help you to discern the voice of God.

God Meets You Where You Are

Even if you don't know a thousand Scriptures, God will speak to you in a way that you can clearly understand. If you are a mathematician, He may speak to you in equations. If you are an artist, He will speak to you in pictures. You won't need someone else to interpret His words. Things that God speaks to you in secret He will also confirm in a hundred different ways. What He says may "coincide" with a message you hear in church, a counseling session with your pastor, a book you are reading, or a poster on the side of a bus. God will make His direction so clear that you couldn't miss it if you tried.

God Never Violates His Word

God is holy. He will not tell you to steal or cheat in order to accomplish His will. What He tells you may have difficult consequences, but in the end God will give you the victory. Be careful not to define the Word of God by one Scripture. Study the full counsel of the Word. A good example is "Bondservants…be obedient to your masters" (Ephesians 6:5). What if a master orders his servant to lie? Should the servant go against the commandment that says he shouldn't practice deceit? Of course not. Pray and ask the Holy Spirit to give you the wisdom to properly discern God's will. It is not only important to understand how God is leading you, it is also important to have a clear sense of His perfect timing.

Be careful not to share what is in your heart with those who are not mature in their faith. The enemy may use them to discourage you from doing what is right.

God Will Not Always Tell You to Do What Seems Logical

When God tells you to do something that doesn't seem practical, He will replace your fear with a peace to let you know that you are on the right track. Don't think He has to do things a certain way. Remember, in the beginning God *created*—He loves to think up creative ways to exercise His perfect will. Behind every great story of victory and success you will find some unusual or miraculous event that probably made no sense at all to human understanding.

Be Sure You Want the Will of God before You Ask for It

Sometimes the will of God may not be what you want to hear. There's a joke about a woman who didn't like the answer she received from God. She promptly responded, "Is there anybody else up there I could talk to?" Many times God will withhold revealing His will because He knows we are not ready to receive it. At other times He will reveal His will knowing that it is not what we want. If we choose to accept the Lord's will, we are also accepting the plan and the reason for which God brought us into the world. But if we choose to disobey, the Lord will find another willing vessel.

ACKNOWLEDGE YOUR HELPER (GOD)

What if the brave woman in our opening story chose not to listen to the voice of God as she made her way through the enemy-infested forest? Suppose she didn't trust the gentle directives of the Holy Spirit? The Bible gives us good advice: "Lean not on your own understanding; / In all your ways acknowledge Him, / And He shall direct your paths" (Proverbs 3:5–6).

The challenge that many contemporary women face is just the opposite of the passive "waiting to be rescued" syndrome. There is such a thing as a woman with a successful career, who routinely makes decisions that will affect the lives of countless people, and who may also provide for and raise children by herself.

This type of woman does not live under the illusion that Prince Charming will come to her rescue. After facing one disappointment after another, she has learned the art of rescuing herself from every situation. She may even be part of the second generation of women left to fend for themselves. The problem is that this woman has a hard time surrendering to her *Ezer*, God.

To make matters even more interesting, we live in a culture that glorifies the myth of the superwoman. Perhaps you've seen the television jingle featuring a woman with the ability to do it all. She sings about how she can run a business, take care of her kids, make dinner, and please her man—"'cause I'm a woman!" In spite of the growing number of women suffering from chronic fatigue, heart attacks, nervous breakdowns, and failed marriages, the social engineers of this nation continue to give three cheers for the woman who proves that she doesn't need anybody's help in order to succeed in life.

From my observations, I can identify three types of women that fit into this category.

The Independent Woman

This woman is so accustomed to taking care of herself she cannot imagine being needy or begging for assistance. If a person upon whom she relies on comes up short in the help department, she immediately shuts down her feelings and takes care of the situation. How long it will take for her to open up again or to rely on someone else depends on the level of her spiritual maturity.

She also faces another challenge—an unintentional one: She tends to vacillate between allowing God to help her and trying to handle everything on her own. In her heart she loves God and knows that God loves her, but she has to constantly remind herself to "let go" of the reins of her life and allow the Lord to take over. She must constantly remind herself of the numerous occasions in which the Lord has demonstrated that He is able and willing to help her and is capable of doing a better job than she.

The Self-Dependent Woman

This woman is stuck in a doctrine of complete reliance upon the actions of the self. In other words, the self-dependent woman is ruled by a spirit of fear that is masked by pride. She will not allow herself to freely accept help from others. She views such offers with the suspicion of a bird rejecting a scrap of bread, fearing it may be a trap. She trusts in her own power when making decisions or taking action.

The self-dependent woman will cry about being alone and not having anyone in her life upon whom she can depend. But try to help this lady and see what you get. No one can pry her hands loose from controlling her relationships, business, or children. God longs to be the *ezer* in her life, but when He—whom the self-dependent woman claims to love—takes too long to act or moves in ways that she doesn't expect, she ignores God's Plan A and immediately goes to Plan H (as in Plan *Her*).

This woman is just as much trouble as the Sleeping Beauty who is waiting to be rescued. Both of these women reject God as the *Ezer* in their lives. Sleeping Beauty looks to a person as her source of salvation; the self-dependent woman has made "self" her god.

The People-Dependent Woman

This woman is a strange mixture of ideas and actions. Contrary to what you might think, the people-dependent woman does not always present herself as the helpless, needy, Sleeping Beauty type. Sometimes she hides her weaknesses and insecurities behind a mask of strength. Instead of being the one needing help, she feeds her neediness by helping others—even to the point of putting her life in jeopardy. She needs people to depend on her in order to affirm her value. She is ruled by what people think of her. She even serves God out of a need to be accepted by Him.

This woman views her good deeds as a way of gaining God's love. She cannot accept the fact that God created her and loves her for who she is, not for what she does. Instead she spends her time and energy rescuing her husband, children, boyfriends, girlfriends, and any family members who might be on alcohol, using drugs, or in financial or emotional trouble. The root of people-dependence may be found in a childhood in which a girl was forced to take on an adult role. Rejection and lack of love and acceptance can also shape a young girl into a people-dependent woman.

Whether she is independent, self-dependent, or people-dependent, this type of woman will move across enemy lines with boldness and confidence, determined to save herself and her village. If she makes it on her own, then she will become even more independent. If she is people-dependent, she will be satisfied with a big dose of approval. If she is self-dependent, she will glory in herself like never before.

That is why I believe God will stand by and allow Miss Anything-but-God-Dependent to fall into a "pit" that is so deep that she cannot rescue herself or anyone else. Her only hope can be found in the hands of the miracle-working *Ezer*.

BECOMING GOD-DEPENDENT

Does God allow overwhelming challenges in order to keep women weak and in their place? Of course not! Such challenges are designed to show us the limitations of human effort. When we face great difficulties, the Lord wants us to operate in the full power of God-dependence. As God-dependent women, we learn that being exalted comes from having humble hearts and that glory comes from complete surrender. The victory comes from complete obedience and reliance upon our heavenly Father.

The woman is our story began her journey as a people-dependent woman. Her life was centered on pleasing her husband. But when she was forced to make a dangerous journey through the forest, she became completely God-dependent.

May I suggest that you take a moment to think about your personality type? How would you define yourself—God-dependent, self-dependent, independent, people-dependent? Husband-dependent, perhaps?

One young lady in my Bible study group described herself as a combination—she moves from one personality type to another. She explained that there are times when she feels truly God-dependent, but she finds that when she is overwhelmed by the pressures of life she moves from God-dependence to independence and sometimes on to people-dependence. She said that when she comes to her senses, she goes back to being God-dependent. But then, when the pressure is on again, she gets frustrated and finds herself repeating the cycle.

The fact is that unless you are willing to go through the process of learning how to become God-dependent, you will find yourself running through the cycles of dependencies like a caged hamster running on a circular treadmill. But if you are serious about taking a stand for the Lord, it is critical that you understand what it means to become totally and fully God-dependent. The following steps are designed to help you reach that end.

Know the Tricks of the Enemy

Our enemy would love to see you fight for your family, your health, your education, your business, or your ministry without complete dependence on the Lord. The one who comes to rob, kill, and destroy would rather you be self-dependent, people-dependent, or independent of God's help. Then he can whip the daylights out of you! This is the source of many of the negative messages we hear in our hearts, messages that say God doesn't care about us, we are not worthy of His love and attention, He doesn't have the power to help us, He is merely a figment of our imagination.

As we become more involved in the Word of God, we soon discover that God sent His Son, Jesus, into the world to seek and save all who were lost. Jesus brought healing and salvation to the demon-possessed, the adulteresses, the sick, the lame, the tax collector, and anyone else who needed His help and deliverance. Knowing the true nature of God as it is revealed in His Word will help you recognize His voice as well as the voice and actions of the enemy.

Know the Power of Spiritual Intimacy

Spiritual intimacy with God builds God-dependence. Without a strong prayer life, we tend to see God as more surreal than tangible. Intimacy in prayer puts "skin" on God.

We must also learn the art of meditating on the things of God. This is a big spiritual step, but I know you can do it. Turn off the television. Turn off your cell phone and beeper. Turn off your car radio, headset, and CD player. Turn off the computer. Turn off your friends. And as you are led by the Lord, turn off your family for a period of time—not once a year, but once a day. (Please stop trembling—you're going to be all right.)

Allow yourself quiet to become "unaware" of your surroundings. Now think on the things of God. Think about His many blessings—how He has protected your life and the lives of your family members. Think about His promises. As you do this, allow yourself to move into the very presence of God.

There will be times when you will not want to quiet yourself in prayer and meditation because then you have to face things that are painful, disturbing, and frustrating. Being still and focused means you have to stop running from your problems. And that's exactly what the Lord wants. He wants you to come quietly to Him, bringing with you all of your fears, your hurts, and your frustrations. He wants to replace your frustrations with sound answers. He wants to replace your fears with His comfort. He wants to take away the heaviness and hurt and replace it with His strength.

As you get to know the Lord in a more intimate way, you will discover that He is not a phantom. Intimacy brings you into a relationship where you come to know God as the One who is fully alive in your mind and heart. When this happens you will become more relaxed, trusting, and God-dependent.

Know God's Track Record of Faithfulness

In order to become God-dependent, you need to understand how faithful God is. Each trial that the Lord brings you through is deisgned to build your faith in Him. As you continue to see the faithfulness of the Lord in ways that are great and small, the enemy will find it harder and harder to lure you back to your old behavior. When you find yourself in a difficult situation, please know that you're in a "fixed fight." God has already given you the victory. Your job is to remain God-dependent. God will use the challenges you face to present you with solid evidence of His faithfulness and power.

There may be times when you don't understand why things turned out differently than you hoped, but in the end you will clearly see that God's way is best. The road of life is like a minefield. There are things buried beneath the surface. One step in the wrong direction might result in a fatal explosion. But the Lord knows every secret of the enemy. He also knows the best direction for your life: "For I know the thoughts that I think toward you, says the LORD, thoughts of peace and not of evil, to give you a future and a hope" (Jeremiah 29:11).

Surround yourself with people who have testimonies of God's faithfulness. If you are battling cancer, ask God to give you a relationship with a cancer survivor. If you are struggling with your ministry, ask the Lord to show you someone who has come through the same struggle. Wisdom and strength can be found in the testimony of an overcomer.

Know That Some Things Are Too Big for You to Handle

I remember visiting my sister years ago. When I arrived in the airport my six-year-old nephew, Todd, ran to greet me. He was very big for his age and he loved to show off his strength. When my suitcase arrived at the baggage claim, he insisted that he wanted to carry it to the car. But when he tried to lift the suitcase, to his dismay it wouldn't budge. Finally I set it upright so it was resting on its wheels. With a little assistance from me, Todd rolled the suitcase to the car. "I told you I could do it!" he said proudly.

God-dependence does not mean that you sit back and do nothing while God handles everything for you. On the other hand, you must not be so impressed with yourself that you misjudge your own strength. Sometimes the will of God for your life seems overwhelming. It doesn't mean that you misunderstood God's plan, or that you should give up or run for cover. It means only that you should do everything humanly possible, and then with a smile on your face step aside and leave the heavy lifting to God.

There may be areas in your life where you are trying to carry things beyond your human strength. Why not close your eyes for a moment and picture a heavy suitcase that is impossible to lift? Then picture the Lord waiting to help you. Try these words: *Lord, I need Your help. I've tried, but I can't carry this load…I release it into Your care.* That's all you need to say. Congratulations! You have just acted as a God-dependent woman!

When all is said and done, the heavy load can be a blessing in disguise. Why? First, it can deepen your faith and your dependency on the Lord. Second, it can build your confidence and esteem because you don't have to prove anything when you know that God's help is readily available. When you are faced with a heavy load, your dependence on God breaks the bonds of fear and anxiety. Then you can say, like the psalmist, "Now I know that the LORD saves His anointed; / He will answer him from His holy heaven with the saving strength of His right hand" (Psalm 20:6).

MY STORY OF GOD-DEPENDENCE

I cannot close this section without telling you the story of a crisis that I faced and how much I needed the Lord to help me. I was facing a very serious matter that was very painful to deal with. I felt betrayed and misused by people I had trusted with all my heart. I had been praying about the matter for some time, but finally the deadline was drawing near and I had to make a decision. It was mid-morning and I was outside walking and praying, which is my daily custom. On this day I labored in prayer as I walked through the park on a deserted road. Finally the Lord spoke to my heart.

He reminded me of a program I had seen on television the night before. It was an interview with a famous British author, whose father had also been a famous author. The two were very close, almost inseparable. When the father died, a great dispute arose over his estate. The son was terrified that he would make a wrong decision and lose everything his father had worked for. One night, as the young man tossed and turned in his sleep, his father appeared to him in a dream. He asked his son why he was so troubled. The son told his father about how he was afraid he would make the wrong decision and lose everything. "If you were here you would know what to do," the young man said.

His father replied, "Don't you realize that you and I are exactly alike? Whatever you choose to do is what I would choose to do, because you and I are one."

His father's image disappeared and the young man was flooded with peace. As I thought about the story, I smiled. Then it was almost as if I could hear the Lord say, *Whatever you choose to do is exactly what I would choose, for you and I are one.*

As I raised my hands in praise and thanksgiving, one of my favorite Scriptures came to mind:

> Be anxious for nothing, but in everything by prayer and supplication, with thanksgiving, let your requests be made known to God; and the peace of God, which surpasses all understanding, will guard your hearts and minds through Christ Jesus. (Philippians 4:6–7)

In spite of sound legal and family advice, I decided not to take action against the person who had wronged me. I was convinced that whatever I decided to do, God would work things out for my good. A few months after making my decision, the person who had treated me unfairly decided to make restitution without any pressure.

The closer we draw to the Lord and the more we strive to stay as one with Him, the more peace we will have about the decisions we make. In spite of what we think about adversity, glorious things begin to happen when we find ourselves surrounded by the enemy. Our faith grows by leaps and bounds and we become more God-dependent as we see the supernatural power of God at work in our lives. It is then we can do the things that "only a woman" can do.

CHAPTER FOUR

Overcoming the Pitfalls

et's return to our story. Early in the morning, just as the woman thought she was out of the woods, she encountered a terrible setback. She fell into a trap set by the enemy. It was a deep, dark pit with smooth walls that made it impossible for her to climb out. No longer could she see the light from the dawning of a new day. There were no more glimpses through the trees of the open field that would lead her to a place where she could find the answer to her prayers in the form of the help she so desperately needed.

What was she thinking as she sat in that dark hole with her faith mortally wounded and the last ounce of hope draining from her soul? She was probably feeling a lot like the psalmist, who brought his complaint before the Lord: "I am like a person without strength—like the slain who lie in the grave. You have laid me in the lowest pit, in darkness, in the depths" (Psalm 88:4–6, paraphrased).

Does the lamenting psalmist blame God for what has happened? Of course! That's what lamentations are all about: to complain and wish bad things on our enemies; to cry out to and plead with God; to blame Him for our troubles; to question His actions; to negotiate with Him.

This raises another question: If you find yourself in a deep pit, is it right to tell God the truth about how you feel? Even if you feel that He has failed you, or betrayed you, or treated you unfairly? After all, isn't He supposed to be the One who protects you from the enemy?[1]

I am persuaded that without honesty we cannot have a real relationship with God—or anyone else. If we cannot vent our feelings to our mates, friends, or coworkers, then our relationships will remain shallow and ineffective. There is no possibility for growth and depth in a relationship where we are denied the right to express our true selves.

The prophet Jeremiah cried out to God that he felt betrayed by Him:

> O LORD, You induced me, and I was persuaded;
>> You are stronger than I, and have prevailed.
> I am in derision daily;
>> Everyone mocks me....
> Then I said, "I will not make mention of Him,
>> Nor speak anymore in His name."
> But His word was in my heart like a burning fire
>> Shut up in my bones;
> I was weary of holding it back,
>> And I could not. (Jeremiah 20:7, 9)

Things got worse for Jeremiah before they got better. Like the woman in our story, he too found himself in a deep pit: "So they took Jeremiah and cast him into the dungeon" (Jeremiah 38:6). This was not God's way of punishing Jeremiah for sharing his true feelings. Rather it was God's way of building Jeremiah's inner strength. "For you have need of endurance, so that after you have done the will of God, you may receive the promise" (Hebrews 10:36). To endure means to suffer but never to surrender.

Eventually, the Lord brought Jeremiah out of the pit filled with more power and endurance than he would ever have thought possible. Afterward, this great prophet wrote a very famous passage of Scripture:

> Through the LORD's mercies we are not consumed,
>   Because His compassions fail not.
> They are new every morning;
>   Great is Your faithfulness. (Lamentations 3:22–23)

I stated earlier that a deep pit can be God's way of bringing us to a place of God-dependence. When there is no way *out,* the miracles are on their way *in.* God can do miracles in a dark pit where everything seems dead and there is no hope of escape. He has the perfect plan for the symbolic pit that is the darkness of our mistakes, our failures, and the circumstance over which we have no control. God can turn the grave-like pit into a life-giving womb in which new character, new revelations, new outlooks, and new visions take shape and are birthed.

Find a woman that is fresh from the pit and you will find a woman that is filled with a God-dependent power that comes only after experiencing the "pitfalls" of life. If a woman claims to have come out of the pit, yet is filled with bitterness and despair, then believe me when I tell you her life is still "the pits."

The woman who has been truly brought back to life from the grave-like pit is fully alive to God and dead to human effort. She is broken, humble, and full of faith. She is joyful, liberated, and ready to do damage for the kingdom of God.

LESSONS FROM THE PIT

Let's take a moment to think about some of the lessons we learn from the "pitfalls" of life.

Life Is Filled with Uncertainties

To put it another way, life is filled with swift transitions. Each of us can point to a time in our lives when some drastic change happened without warning. Still, we are surprised when our best-laid plans are sometimes interrupted or intercepted. God sees the unforeseen, and He knows the effect it will have on us.

If you're wondering whether this means you shouldn't make any long-term plans—because after all, you never know what might happen next—I don't think that's what God had in mind. I believe that we should definitely have short- and long-term goals. But we must remember that even when we work hard to make things better, God is two steps ahead, working things out not for the better, but for the best.

To keep us from feeling overwhelmed, the Lord unfolds His plan slowly. To us it may feel like a dramatic turn of events, but in the eternal realm the "turn of events" has always been a part of God's plan for us. That's why the Lord wants us to be prepared for change.

The best advice I ever received about handling the uncertainties of life came from Pastor E. V. Hill, who led me to the Lord and helped me to mature in my faith. Pastor Hill often said, "Wear positions, titles, and material things like a loose garment. Never wrap them tightly around you. For if the Lord should call you to release certain things—or things choose to release you—it is easier to let go if you're not wrapped up in them."

The apostle Paul put it this way:

> Not that I speak in regard to need, for I have learned in whatever state I am, to be content: I know how to be abased [live humbly], and I know how to abound [live in abundance]. Everywhere and in all things I have learned both to be full and to be hungry, both to abound and to suffer need. (Philippians 4:11–12, emphasis and insertions mine)

To be sure, dealing with the uncertainties of life is a learning process. No one wants to volunteer for an overnight stay in the pit, but if you should find yourself in a deep hole looking up at the sky, realize it just might be a blessing in disguise.

We Must Move from Fear to Faith

Fear can leave us paralyzed in the face of an enemy attack. There is no doubt that fear is one of Satan's greatest tools in keeping us from experiencing God's will for our lives.

Fear tells you in a thousand subtle ways that no matter how many times you try, you will fail. The voice of fear tells you there is no one who can save you from a terrible fate. Once you begin to believe the voice, you put into motion the psychological machinery that will work full time to usher you into the failure and destruction that Satan desires you to experience.

Fear can mask itself as a sudden illness, an accident, or some other catastrophe. If fear is not overcome, it will cause you to self-destruct or quietly bow out of the plan that God has for your life.

According to the Word of God, the greatest weapon against fear is love. "There is no fear in love; but perfect love casts out fear" (1 John 4:18). The marvelous mystery of perfect love casting out fear is completely solved just a few verses earlier: "He who does not love does not know God, for God is love" (1 John 4:8). If it is true that God is *love* and that perfect *love* casts out fear, then it is *God* that casts out fear.

When love becomes more important than your own life, it becomes perfect love. Allow me to explain. Picture a woman who is afraid of water and cannot swim. She and her young child are walking by a lake. Suddenly the child trips and falls into the water. The woman's love for that child will override her fear of water. Even though she cannot swim and there is no one to help her, she will jump into the water and attempt to save her child. Scripture tells us,

"...for love is as strong as death" (Song of Solomon 8:6). The woman cannot swim, but the strength of her love conquers her fears and stirs her faith. Without a strong love for God, it is not possible to develop a strong faith in God.

Only the love that comes from God can give you the power you need to crush your fears underfoot and allow you to reach your desired end. Human love is wonderful, but its power is limited. To draw from an endless supply of power and love, you must have an "uplink" to the love of God. (More about God's uplink in a later chapter.) God's love comes with a written guarantee that it will never run out.

> For He Himself has said, "I will never leave you nor forsake
>   you."
> So we may boldly say:
>   "The Lord is my helper;
> I will not fear.
>   What can man do to me?" (Hebrews 13:5b–6)

God uses the challenges we face to demonstrate the enduring power and faithfulness of His love. It is the indwelling power of God's love that moves us toward greater faith. Love is the match we strike to cause our faith to burn brightly. As God shapes us into women of love and power, faith must become our way of life.

We Must Watch and Pray

One of the things I enjoy most is taking a daily walk on a mountain trail not far from my house. The challenge that comes with walking in a wooded area is that from time to time you might run across creepy-crawlers—snakes and such. I really enjoy praying at the top of the hill that overlooks the city, but believe me, after running across rattlesnakes on two separate occasions, one of which was politely blocking my path, I have learned to watch as I pray.

There are times when the enemy catches us off guard. That's exactly what happened to me. I was taking one of my early morning walks with a friend. Halfway up the trail we met a woman who was also heading up the trail. We started talking and in the course of our conversation she mentioned a beautiful pool at the top of the mountain. I had heard about this mountain pool, but I wasn't sure where it was located. My friend and I decided to take the stranger up on her offer to show us this beautiful sight at the top of the mountain.

We were still laughing and talking as we followed the woman up the hill and onto a narrow path, thick with foliage on both sides. When we finally came to a clearing, we found ourselves standing on the edge of a cliff with a sixty-foot drop below us. The path was so narrow that it was impossible to turn around. "Don't look down," the woman said cheerfully as she made her way along the narrow ledge.

I'm not sure whether I was holding onto God's hand or a long tree root that was growing on the side of the mountain—I was too afraid to look. Whatever it was, I was praying hard as I inched my way along the unstable cliff, the dirt ledge crumbling beneath my feet. Finally I made it back to solid ground. The hairs on my arms still rise when I think about how a strange woman led us onto that cliff. I might add that I was so angry at the devil after that experience that I witnessed to the woman until she came to the Lord.

We must be on guard at all times. Our culture is filled with all kinds of deceptive pitfalls. One unforeseen crisis and a solid marriage can end in divorce court. Singles get involved in sexual promiscuity, sometimes with deadly consequences. Children are being enticed by drugs and by alternative lifestyles.

Jesus gave us one very uncomplicated solution to the challenge of uncertainties. "Watch therefore, and pray always that you may be

counted worthy to escape all these things that will come to pass"
(Luke 21:36a). Many of the pitfalls in life are not God's plan for us.
They come as a result of our lack of awareness and prayer. It is time
to pay closer attention to the decisions we make and to the people
whom we allow into our lives.

Watch and pray over your marriage. Pray for your mate daily. Listen
more and talk less. Don't hope for more time with your family—
instead, plan time together. Watch and pray regarding conflicts in
schools and in the workplace. Watch and pray for the person you
are dating or planning to marry. Watch and pray over your children.
Don't allow them to become entangled in popular trends. Be careful
whom you allow to watch your children. Watch and pray over
things related to ministry. If you are not prayerful, the devil will slip
in and undermine the work of God.

Last but not least, watch and pray for yourself. Watch and pray
over your decisions, big and little. Take a good look at your behavior. Ask God to show you your inner self. King David said, "Search
me, O God, and know my heart; / Try me, and know my anxieties;
/ And see if there is any wicked way in me" (Psalm 139:23–24a).

I encourage you to slow down, break your busy routine, and
watch (with the eyes of the Spirit) the things that are going on
around you. As God exposes that which was hidden, pray for guidance about how to handle those things.

PRAYERS FOR PEOPLE EXPERIENCING PITFALLS

Different kinds of prayer are effective for women that are trapped in
pits. Consider these:

Devotional Prayer

This kind of prayer should be done on a daily basis. If your schedule and your temperament allow, early morning is the best time for
devotional prayer. Morning prayer helps to prepare you for the

things you will encounter during the course of the day. Let me remind you that God is alive and that He is the source of your life. God doesn't want pager messages or e-mails from us; He wants relationships. Guard your heart against coming to the Lord with thoughts like these: *Dear Lord, today I ask that you let my boss be in a good mood when I get to the office. And please, Lord, touch my husband's heart so we can take that trip to visit my family...blah, blah, blah.*

One morning I made the mistake of praying one of those rude prayers. The Lord immediately interrupted me and said, *I'm not an answering service. Don't leave me a message! I'm here with you, so treat me with the same respect you would show to a dear friend.* I stopped in my tracks and thought about a verse that says, "Enter into His gates with thanksgiving, and into His courts with praise" (Psalm 100:4). I immediately began to give thanks to the Lord and to praise Him for His goodness and kindness. I became so caught up in praising the Lord that all of the things I'd meant to tell Him—the things I'd meant to ask Him for—grew strangely dim. We just enjoyed being together like two good friends.

Stop and think: Wouldn't it be rude and insensitive to pour out your heart to a friend, then to walk away without finding out what she might need to share with you? I think you catch my drift. Devotional prayer is spending time with someone you love and who loves you. That special someone is your heavenly Father.

Intercessory Prayer

This is praying for special needs, such as other people or critical situations. Sometimes you may choose to accompany this type of prayer with a time of fasting or consecration. This means to choose, for a set period of time, to restrict yourself to nonessential activities. You might set a limited diet, such as juices and fruits and vegetables, or even go without food altogether. Prayers for your mate, your children, or another person that is close to your heart can find added strength when you fast and consecrate yourself while you pray.

Intercession may also be a time of joining with others in praying for similar needs. There is a great release of power when dedicated women of God come together in prayer. The ministry of intercession can literally change the face of our world. Women should band together to pray godly leaders back into positions of authority. Women should stand in prayer against the evil forces that are at work in our society. Women praying together can release the spirit of healing and deliverance to suffering people. The possibilities are endless.

Not only does intercession help others, it also grows women into greater spiritual authority. All women should search out and connect to a mature prayer partner or to a small prayer group in which intercession can be made on behalf of this nation's needs and for special people that are placed on their hearts.

Meditative Prayer

This is a special time of separation for the purpose of fellowship and intimacy with God. Let me clear one thing up for you: Meditation does not belong to the New Age movement. Over and over again the Bible tells us to meditate on the things of God.

> This Book of the Law shall not depart from your mouth, but you shall meditate in it day and night, that you may observe to do according to all that is written in it. For then you will make your way prosperous, and then you will have good success. (Joshua 1:8)

Somewhere along the line Christians found themselves too busy to spend long periods of time basking in the presence of God and meditating on His Word. This could be the reason why so many believers are not experiencing "good success."

In the last twenty years, the New Age movement has borrowed

the practice of meditation (minus the Word of God) and placed it at the center of their theology. But the true idea of meditation is a time of spiritual refreshment, of drawing strength from the power of God, and of hearing God's voice in a way that brings revelation and direction. Meditative prayer can be for a few hours or a few days.

Take a long drive, spend the day at the beach, or retreat into a quiet room. There is no set agenda except the need for more of God. It is a time of focusing on the Scriptures—not as something you study as a task like college reading—in a way that allows the Lord to give insight to His Word. When you spend time in meditative prayer, sitting quietly and thinking about the things of God, you will have more power to discern the will and the ways of God.

Warfare Prayer

This is a special area of prayer that is not designed for spiritual babes. Sometimes circumstances force you to hold on to the "coattails" of the Spirit as you plunge into the waters of deep prayer.

The Scriptures give us an example of people in need of warfare prayer:

> Others went out on the sea in ships; they were merchants
>   on the mighty waters.
> They saw the works of the LORD, his wonderful deeds in the
>   deep…
> In their peril their courage melted away.
> They reeled and staggered like drunken men; they were at
>   their wits' end. (Psalm 107:23–24, 26–27, NIV)

In the original language, "wits' end" means, "All their wisdom was swallowed up." Coming to your wits' end is a good opportunity for God to show you the real power of prayer. Those of you who are in need of a spiritual breakthrough—that are struggling with illness, spiritual attack, or persecution—are prime candidates for the school of warfare prayer, which is run exclusively by the Holy Spirit.

When the rug has been pulled out from under you and you find yourself suspended in midair, hoping that the invisible hand of God will hold you up, you are in a brave new world. Your mind no longer has the ability to think what to pray. The Spirit takes over and your words turn into groans:

> Likewise the Spirit also helps in our weaknesses. For we do not know what we should pray for as we ought, but the Spirit Himself makes intercession for us with groanings which cannot be uttered. (Romans 8:26)

In warfare prayer you do not *choose* to fast, you simply become numb to the needs of your flesh. You feel suspended in time and the only need is be filled with more of God's presence. Fasting comes without effort when you are overflowing with the Spirit of the Lord. When your level of prayer takes you into a realm where you lose all desire for natural food and pleasure, prayer becomes powerful and effective.

Once you have seen His "wonders in the deep"—even the deep pit—and have become fully aware that there is a level of prayer in which Satan can be defeated, you move to a more powerful level in all areas of your prayer life.

Let me remind you that we are in the midst of an invisible war with an enemy that hopes we will be totally unprepared to deal with the uncertainties of this life. But these pits are never without meaning or value. The Lord has given us the tools of survival and escape: Abandon fear, become full of faith, meditate, and pray. Like Jeremiah, tell God how you feel. Then praise Him for His unfailing compassion.

You are like the clay on the potter's wheel. The Lord desires to shape you into a vessel of honor. Don't resist…. Yield.

CHAPTER FIVE

Facing the Enemy

et's return to our opening story. It was not by chance but through the miraculous intervention of the Lord that the woman's baby cried out just as the soldier raised his weapon to kill his enemy. As the woman and her child were pulled from the dark pit, her mind filled with fear. What would she say if the soldier asked why she was in the forest? She tried to think, but her mind was blank. Just as she emerged from the dark hole, a voice whispered to her:

> When they deliver you up, do not worry about how or what you should speak. For it will be given to you in that hour what you should speak; for it is not you who speak, but the Spirit of your Father who speaks in you. (Matthew 10:19–20)

The woman bowed at the soldier's feet. She was overcome with a strange mixture of fear and joy—joy because she'd been rescued from the pit, and fear of what would happen if the soldier suspected that she was on a mission to save her village. She swallowed her panic, prayed for wisdom, then poured out her heart.

"Thank God, kind sir, for showing mercy to me and my child. If you tell me your name, when my son comes of age I will tell to him the story of the brave soldier who rescued us from the hands of death."

The soldier was so taken with the woman's gracious speech that he gave her a fresh supply of bread and water for her journey and showed her the path that was free of hidden traps.

I would love to know what you are feeling as you read this part of the story. What do you think of the woman's behavior when she encountered the soldier? Did you see her as groveling, whining, or faking gratitude? How would you have handled an encounter with someone who had the power to take your life? Would you have stood fearlessly in the face of the enemy and said, "Go ahead—make my day"? Or would you have responded as this woman did? Could it be that by praising the soldier the woman appealed to his heroic nature? If she had challenged him, would that have caused him to be defensive and treat her like an enemy? In truth, I'm not sure if any of us know what we would do if we were face-to-face with a real enemy.

The woman's choice of behavior makes a very important point. As women, two of the greatest weapons we have against our enemies are ones we seldom use anymore: the weapons of *graciousness* and *favor*. How did we come to a place in our culture where, in the face of adversity, we have replaced the art of being a gracious woman with martial arts and manipulation? Self-defense has its place, but does the contemporary woman think that being gracious is a sign of weakness? Does she think that going "toe-to-toe" with the opposition brings better and quicker results? Or is it a lack of understanding that turns a woman's attitude and tongue into weapons that usually bring negative results?

The Bible says, "A soft answer turns away wrath, but a harsh word stirs up anger" (Proverbs 15:1). When my grandmother, Sadie Bell Campbell, was alive, she used to say, "Words laced with honey work better than words laced with vinegar."

Whatever you do, please don't confuse being gracious with using sex appeal to get what you want. There is a vast difference between sex appeal and graciousness. Sex appeal is only effective with those who may find you sexually attractive. Unfortunately, enemies usually come in a broad variety. Sex appeal is the idea of a woman using the promise of sexual intimacy as a negotiating tool. The gracious woman, on the other hand, would never compromise her integrity as a woman. She makes her appeal to her enemies in the spirit of family or as a cherished friend.

The Old Testament includes a story about a woman named Abigail. She was a classic example of a gracious woman. The Scriptures tell us that she was "of good understanding and beautiful" (1 Samuel 25:3). But Abigail was married to a foolish man, Nabal, who made the mistake of insulting King David—the one who killed the giant Goliath and annihilated the Philistines, remember? When David and his soldiers were on their way to repay Nabal for his evil deeds, Abigail intercepted and became her husband's strong *ezer*.

I hope you don't doze off and miss what I am about to say. This may sound old-fashioned, but it's true: *Food still works!* Abigail's servants prepared a generous peace offering of two hundred loaves of bread, two barrels of wine, five dressed sheep, and bushels of raisin cakes and grain. With the most gracious words she could find, Abigail pleaded for the lives of her husband and his men. David, who was probably hungry, was so moved by her eloquent speech and her generous offering that he spared the lives of her husband and of all his men.

THE QUALITIES OF A GRACIOUS WOMAN

As Abigail's story so clearly illustrates, a gracious woman is like a cool oasis in a dry land. She calms the angry, refreshes the weary, and strengthens the weak. A gracious woman is like a weapon that is so powerful yet pleasant that enemies are defeated with smiles on their faces.

I think it's time for women to relearn the art of being gracious. To do that, we need to understand what graciousness is—and isn't.

Never Mistake Being Gracious for Being Fearful

A fearful woman falls apart under pressure. A gracious woman maintains her composure.

Never Mistake Being Gracious for Being Passive

A passive woman refuses to act because she is afraid of the consequences. A gracious woman may not take immediate action. She first seeks wisdom; then she will act.

Never Mistake Being Gracious for Being Foolish

A foolish woman will take rash action and make senseless choices to save herself. A gracious woman will show kindness to her enemy so that her attack will come as a surprise.

Never Mistake Being Gracious for Being Naive

A naive woman is poorly informed about her enemy. A gracious woman will listen quietly in order to gather critical information. She never takes action without understanding what she's up against.

Never Mistake Being Gracious for Being Outdated

A contemporary women is prone to try new, unproven techniques to deal with age-old problems. The gracious woman looks for tools that have been tried and proven successful.

Never Mistake Being Gracious for Weakness

Some men and some feminists view gentle, kind, gracious behavior in the midst of crisis as female weakness. But the Bible tells us that the Lord is gracious and full of compassion. Kings, queens, ambassadors, and people in business and in authority master the art of being gracious in order to survive.

Never Mistake Being Gracious for Being Powerless

A woman that is kind, compassionate, and slow to act in the face of adversity causes those lacking in wisdom to underestimate her power. But hiding beneath her soft voice and kind smile may be a woman that has fasted and prayed and is full of the power of the Holy Spirit.

THE QUALITIES OF A WOMAN WITH FAVOR

There is no greater biblical example of a woman with favor than Esther. I fondly refer to the book of Esther as the book of Queens, since it is the only book in the Bible that is centered around two women, both of whom were queens. The first was Queen Vashti. She lost the favor of her husband, King Xerxes, and was replaced by a young Jewish woman named Esther. This young woman was carried on the wings of the Spirit to a very special place in history.

After her parents died, she was adopted by her uncle Mordecai. (Please note that women of real substance have usually been humbled by personal adversity. Sometimes, as with Esther, it happens at a very early age.) Jewish historians write that Esther was rounded up with the other beautiful women and taken to the king's palace against her will. A Jewish woman would not willingly have married outside of her race.

After Esther was taken, her uncle warned her to hide her racial origin because of the hatred against the Jewish people. In a whirlwind of events, Xerxes fell in love with Esther and crowned her queen of the Persian empire. Little did Esther know that as she settled into a life of comfort and safety that her true destiny was to become the *ezer* of the Jewish people.

Many theologians believe it was Esther's great beauty that won the heart of the king. But when time permits, grab your Bible and take a closer look at the book of Esther. It reads, "The young woman was lovely and beautiful" (Esther 2:7). The word *lovely* comes from the Hebrew *tov*.[1] This word has nothing to do with physical appearance. It refers to the beauty of the heart. *Tov* can be translated as "pleasing, delightful, agreeable, and radiant favor."

Without a doubt, Esther was more than a pretty face. She had an asset that set her apart from the other women. The sweet fragrance of her character drew people to her and gave her a special place in their hearts.

How do we define the word *favor?* Let me begin by saying that favor begins with a favorable attitude. A woman with this kind of disposition is easygoing and likable. She is not fussy or hard to please. She does not think more of herself than she should. She is grateful to God and to people for their kindness. She never takes things for granted.

Esther could have been arrogant because of her great beauty, but I am certain that as she looked around at all of the other beautiful women, she recognized that only the grace of God would allow her to prevail. So she cooperated fully and humbled herself with the king's eunuch, Hegai. She took his advice and never asked for special treatment. In the midst of a group of spoiled and demanding women, Esther's favorable attitude made her a shining star. Favor is not something that you learn, it's a gift. Esther had the gift of favor long before she ever set foot in the king's palace.

Favor may be bestowed upon someone that, unbeknownst to the bearer, has been called to do a special work for the Lord. Favor is a special gift that is given to those with a deep love for the Lord that spend time in His presence.

The throne room of God is filled with a powerful, radioactive material called favor. The more time you spend in the presence of

God, the more radiant you become and the sweeter your disposition and attitude will be. When the favor of God is upon you, it causes you to shine. You stand out in a crowd. The sound of your name is sweet to the ear.

When you delight in spending time in the presence of the Lord, He will cover you with favor. We see this demonstrated in Jesus, who "increased in wisdom and stature, and in favor with God and men" (Luke 2:52).

GRACIOUSNESS AND FAVOR AT WORK

As the empress of Persia, Esther soon came face-to-face with a deadly enemy. His name was Haman and his plan was to destroy all of the Jews in the Babylonian empire. Esther became God's instrument of deliverance by using two simple yet powerful weapons: graciousness and favor. She never lost her composure. She never used force or made demands. Instead she prayed and fasted.

> Go, gather all the Jews who are present in Shushan, and fast for me; neither eat nor drink for three days, night or day. My maids and I will fast likewise. (Esther 4:16a)

Esther, along with all the other Jewish people, entered into a time of fasting that was highly honored by the Lord. The Lord directed Esther to prepare a feast for the king and for Haman, the enemy of the Jews. You can almost hear the psalm of David playing softly in the background as Esther planned her special banquet. "You prepare a table before me in the presence of my enemies; You anoint my head with oil; My cup runs over" (Psalm 23:5). Oh, how awesome to confront your enemies when you have been anointed with the perfumed oil of favor, for "favor is better than silver and gold" (Proverbs 22:1, NASB).

Every woman should know how to make herself look attractive, regardless of age, size, or income. Every woman should know how to prepare an anointed meal and entertain guests. But without the favor of the Lord, all of our human efforts are like a house of cards. When the Lord prepares a table—or a corporate desk or doctor's office—in the presence of a woman's enemies, if she has a covenant relationship with the Lord, she can depend on His favor to be in full operation and His will to be accomplished.

Esther shows us something else as well. Please don't make the mistake of thinking your enemies will stay safely tucked away on the other side of town or in another city. No, my dear ones, enemies like Haman come very close indeed. They shake your hand, kiss your cheek, engage you in conversation, and wish you well—all the while circling like vultures, planning your destruction. When it comes to confronting your enemies you must be "wise as serpents and harmless as doves" (Matthew 10:16).

The word *favor* is used seven times in relation to Esther. I have listed them so you can see for yourself how powerfully God used the spirit of favor to allow Esther to save the Jewish nation.

> Esther also was taken to the king's palace, into the care of Hegai the custodian of the women. Now the young woman pleased him, and she obtained his *favor*; so he readily gave beauty preparations to her, besides her allowance. (Esther 2:8b–9a)

> Now when the turn came for Esther…to go in to the king, she requested nothing but what Hegai the king's eunuch, the custodian of the women, advised. And Esther obtained *favor* in the sight of all who saw her. (2:15)

> The king loved Esther more than all the other women, and she obtained grace and *favor* in his sight more than all the

virgins; so he set the royal crown upon her head and made her queen instead of Vashti. (2:17)

So it was, when the king saw Queen Esther standing in the court, that she found *favor* in his sight.... And the king said to her, "What do you wish, Queen Esther? What is your request? It shall be given to you—up to half my kingdom!" (5:2–3)

Then Esther answered and said, "My petition and request is this: If I have found *favor* in the sight of the king, and if it pleases the king to grant my petition and fulfill my request, then let the king and Haman come to the banquet." (5:7–8a)

Then Queen Esther answered and said, "If I have found *favor* in your sight, O king, and if it pleases the king, let my life be given me at my petition, and my people at my request." (7:3)

If it pleases the king, and if I have found *favor* in his sight and the thing seems right to the king and I am pleasing in his eyes, let it be written to revoke the letters devised by Haman, the son of Hammedatha the Agagite, which he wrote to annihilate the Jews who are in all the king's provinces."

[The king replied to Esther and Mordecai:] "You yourselves write a decree concerning the Jews, as you please, in the king's name, and seal it with the king's signet ring; for whatever is written in the king's name and sealed with the king's signet ring no one can revoke." (8:5, 8)

Isn't it good to know that just like Abigail and Esther, as well as the woman in our opening story, we are not without help when we face our enemies? We can learn from their examples to be gracious to those who oppose us, and to seek the gift of favor by delighting in the Lord. Then when the King of kings makes a decree to protect us and seals it with His word, it can never be revoked. "I will call upon the LORD, who is worthy to be praised; So shall I be saved from my enemies" (Psalm 18:3).

CHAPTER SIX

Presenting Your Petition

want you to picture the woman in our opening story as she arrives at her destination. She is exhausted. Her skin is grimy and covered in sweat. Her hair is disheveled and her clothes are dirty from her fall into the pit. Her baby won't stop crying. The people in the neighboring village don't know what to make of this strange woman as she staggers toward the men guarding the gate.

"Please," she says over her crying baby. "I must talk to the elders."

After she has pleaded desperately with one of the guards, he finally goes to the counsel of elders and tells them the woman's story. The woman sits beneath a tree, too tired to pray or to think. Someone touches her shoulder and leads her to where the group of men have gathered.

"Why should we help you?" the leader demands. His tone seems harsh, almost cruel. The woman had already gone through so much—to hear what sounds like rejection in his voice makes her want to scream. She wants to pick up a rock and throw it at the men for being so stupid. Finally, as her child falls asleep, something inside of the woman's spirit also grows peaceful. She weeps as she realizes that it isn't up to her to convince the elders to help her—it is up to the Lord. The entire matter rests in His hands.

There's an important principle that we must be aware of when presenting a critical petition. The best way to help you understand what I am trying to say is to tell you about a terrifying telephone call I received from my daughter one evening. She called from her house, screaming at the top of her lungs, "Mom, come quick! Please, help me!"

My heart was pounding with fear as I asked, "What's wrong?" I gripped the telephone tightly with one hand and searched for my car keys with the other.

There was a long pause, then a deep sob. "There's a lizard in my house!"

I can't begin to tell you how relieved I was to know that her house wasn't on fire. She had not suffered a terrible accident; no one had broken in and hurt her. She was furious when I let out a peal of laughter and sent my nephew to her rescue. For me the whole matter had turned into a comic moment, although my daughter was so terrified that she refused to sleep in her house for weeks.

In many instances we present our emergency petitions to God with the same lack of perspective. What terrifies us and sends us to our knees in 9-1-1 prayer causes God to shake His head and comment to the heavenly host, *It's no big deal.*

On the other hand, we may come to God with an everyday matter and have God sound the alarms of heaven. We might view a matter as unimportant, but the Lord sees what the enemy attempts to conceal.

Say you're dead tired and you whisper a prayer asking God to keep you safe before boarding a plane. Suddenly you get bumped off the flight and you're furious. But didn't you just ask the Lord to protect you? To you it's not an emergency situation, but the Lord sees the danger and moves heaven and earth to keep you from boarding that flight.

No matter how desperate your situation may appear, when you

are presenting your petition or making your request known to God, remember that he is all-seeing and all-knowing. As a believer, your responsibility is not to panic—put your complete trust, confidence, and hope in God. Where there is hope, there is power to cope with whatever life brings. The psalmist put it this way:

> Deliver me, O my God, out of the hand of the wicked,
>> Out of the hand of the unrighteous and cruel man.
> For You are my hope, O Lord GOD,
>> You are my trust from my youth. (Psalm 71:4–5)

The following ideas can help you experience peace that passes all understanding as you present your petition to the Lord.

DON'T BE DISCOURAGED
IF AT FIRST YOU GET A NEGATIVE RESPONSE

In the book of Matthew is a story about a woman from Canaan who desperately tried to get Jesus to hear her plea. "Have mercy on me, O Lord, Son of David! My daughter is severely demon-possessed" (Matthew 15:22b). Jesus responded to the woman in a manner that was almost insulting. He made it clear that He had no intention of giving her the help she needed: "But He answered and said, 'It is not good to take the children's bread and throw it to the little dogs'" (v. 26).

Does this answer surprise you? After all, Jesus was the champion of the helpless. He was known for His compassion. Best of all, He was a miracle-working Savior. So if He turned the woman down, there was nowhere else for her to turn for help.

There are times when the Lord will test our faith and perseverance by refusing to respond to our petitions in the way we think He should. He's not a genie in a bottle! God uses such experiences to build spiritual character. For example, the Bible tells us that "God resists the proud, but gives grace to the humble" (1 Peter 5:5). When it appears that you are not a recipient of God's favor, the Lord monitors the attitude of your heart. Humility draws Him; pride repels Him.

The Canaanite woman passed the humility test with flying colors. She should have been completely discouraged when Jesus publicly rejected her petition, but desperate times call for desperate measures. In spite of what was said, she refused to give up. Her need was so great that she couldn't afford to allow embarrassment or rejection to get the best of her. Her faith rose within her and she found the words that opened Jesus' heart. "And she said, 'Yes, Lord, yet even the little dogs eat the crumbs which fall from their masters' table'" (Matthew 15:27).

Jesus was so impressed by the woman's faith and humility that He honored her petition. "O woman, great is your faith! Let it be to you as you desire" (v. 28).

The Canaanite woman gives us a wonderful lesson of faith in action. Even when it appears that you are not going to get the help you need, it is as a great philosopher once said: "It's not over 'til it's over." I like to think of it this way: It's not over 'til *God* says it's over!

When you present your petition to the Lord, you must stand in faith and believe that your needs will be met. No matter how dark things look, know He will keep you. "Without faith it is impossible to please God" (Hebrews 11:6, NIV).

DON'T BE DISCOURAGED
WHEN THE ANSWER YOU SEEK TAKES TIME

The woman in our story stood before the elders. She listened as they debated with one another, trying to decide what to do about her petition. While the men scratched their heads and paced back and forth, all she could think about was her dying husband and the people who were at that very moment being attacked by the enemy.

No doubt you have been in a situation in which every minute seemed critical, yet where there were forms to fill out, people who needed to be consulted, miles of red tape to wade through, and piles of excuses to answer. *Lord, I'm running out of time! What are You doing? Why can't You help me find a way around all of this nonsense?*

Two sisters named Mary and Martha were once also in a race against time. Their brother was dying. When they sent a message to Jesus asking for His help, the last thing they needed was a delay. "Therefore the sisters sent to Him, saying, 'Lord, behold, he whom You love is sick'" (John 11:3).

Logic says that if someone you love is sick, you rush to his side—especially if you have the power to heal him. Right? Listen to how Jesus handled the emergency. "So, when He heard that he was sick, He stayed two more days in the place where He was" (v. 6).

There is no worse feeling than to need the Lord's divine intervention at a particular time and to find Him seemingly absent. Because of my personal experiences, I know how Mary and Martha must have felt when their brother drew his last breath. Where was Jesus? Nowhere in sight. But when Father God looked at the heavenly clock, He saw that everything was moving along according to His perfect schedule. In spite of how things appeared on earth, He had a plan for Mary, Martha, and Lazarus. Jesus showed up when His Father told Him it was time. Of course, Mary and Martha had no idea what God was doing. Just like me, they were saying to themselves, *My God, My God, why have You forsaken me?*

Actually, Martha had quite a few words for Jesus: "Lord, if You had been here, my brother would not have died. But even now I know that whatever You ask of God, God will give You" (John 11:21–22). Allow me to give my personal translation of what Martha was saying: "You were supposed to be my brother's best friend and You let him die. Now I want you to talk to God and ask Him to work a miracle. Because I want my brother back and I want him back now!"

The thing I love most about the Lord is that while He knows all about the big picture of what He is trying to accomplish, He is also aware of the small picture that fills my imagination and causes me to spin out of control in frustration and anxiety. He offers me peace instead of panic—if I will accept it.

God carried out His plan according to His timeframe even though Martha and Mary went through tremendous pain and agony thinking that Jesus had forsaken them. Most people know the story of how Jesus raised Lazarus from the dead. What most people don't understand, though, is why the Lord waited until Lazarus was dead for three days before coming to his rescue.

The mystery of why Jesus allowed His friend Lazarus to experience the grave is connected to the beliefs of the Jewish people. The Jews believe that it takes three days for the spirit to depart from the body before a person is officially dead. If the person wakes up before the three-day period is over, then it is clear that that person has been in what we refer to today as a coma.

Jesus intentionally waited until Lazarus was officially dead, buried, and decaying, so that people from that time forward would know that God has the power to handle the most seemingly impossible situation. When Jesus raised the dead, there was a new understanding when it came to presenting a prayer petition: With God *all* things are possible.

After facing several personal crises in which God-delays caused my faith to waver, I finally got the message. This is what I felt the Lord was saying to me on a night when I cried out, telling Him I couldn't stand another day of what I was going through: *Delays are the servants of My perfect timing.*

When you get ahead of God's perfect plan for your life, He holds back the tide by introducing delay. No matter where you turn or how hard you try to wrestle or move the obstacle, delay creates the perfect blockade that keeps you from reaching your desired end. Delay looks toward heaven, waiting for the signal from God.

"Is it time yet?" Delay calls out to God.

"Not yet!" God answers. "I'm still preparing her heart. I'm still preparing the perfect person and circumstance."

In the fullness of time, and usually when you are least expecting it, God answers your petition.

"Delay, your work is finished. No more hindrances!" God calls out.

Delay looks to the Lord. "I will release my grip and allow the blessings to flow."

"Blessings, it is time!" the Lord commands. "Come forth in full abundance!"

You Must Surrender Your Desires

Have you ever had a need so deep that you didn't know where to turn or what to do? Like the woman who was trying to save her village, you may know what it's like to be a grimy mess with your problems screaming so loud that your petition can hardly be heard over all the noise and confusion. You are literally at your wits' end.

In the first chapter of 1 Samuel, a woman named Hannah was heartbroken because she had no children. In old testament times it was a curse for a woman not to have children. Needless to say, Hannah suffered tremendous ridicule because of her barrenness— especially from her husband's second wife, who had already given birth to several children. Hannah cried and fasted, but still the Lord did not allow her to have a child. The book of James gives a possible clue as to why Hannah's prayer was not answered: "You ask and do not receive, because you ask amiss, that you may spend it on your pleasures" (James 4:3).

It is clear that from the beginning that Hannah's desire for a male child represented much more than a woman's natural desire to have children. When Hannah prayed, why didn't she ask the Lord for a healthy child, male or female? The answer can be found in the pages of Jewish culture and belief. Every Jewish woman hoped that by having a son the Messiah might spring from her line. Hannah wanted not only to silence the unbearable taunting of her husband's second wife, but to gain the acceptance and status that came with giving birth to a male child.

Hannah refused to be comforted by the blessings that surrounded her. She had a husband who loved her dearly, who gave her everything she wanted or needed. In spite of all she had, Hannah was obsessed with the one thing she didn't have.

If you keep digging you will find even more secret motives that may have kept the Lord from honoring Hannah's petition. Thoughts of having a child completely ruled her heart. The desire for a child became a symbol of the very thing that was keeping God from being first in Hannah's life. We all must be careful that the things we desire do not completely rule our hearts. God will not sit in a corner while our desires have free rein.

The thing you're longing for may be a husband, a better job, a college degree, money, a business of your own, or whatever has the potential of being more important to you than your relationship with the Lord. Hannah's husband takes his words from the mouth of God when he sees the level of his wife's sorrow and discontentment: "Then Elkanah her husband said to her, 'Hannah, why do you weep? Why do you not eat? And why is your heart grieved? Am I not better to you than ten sons?'" (1 Samuel 1:8).

God intends for His love to fill us so completely that every other gift life brings is simply added joy. When you claim to have a relationship with the Lord yet are drowning in a sea of unfulfilled desires, the Lord wants to know, as did Elkanah, "Why do you weep? Why do you not eat? And why is your heart grieved? Am I not better than ten of those things?"

I am not certain how Hannah came to release her greatest desire to the Lord. Maybe the pain and frustration became so unbearable that she finally realized she had to set herself free from the source of her torment. So in one final act of desperation, she went to the house of prayer and surrendered to God the very thing she wanted most.

> Then she made a vow and said, "O LORD of hosts, if You will indeed look on the affliction of Your maidservant and remember me, and not forget Your maidservant, but will give Your maidservant a male child, then I will give him to the LORD all the days of his life." (1 Samuel 1:11)

Isn't it amazing how we want so much from God, but seldom think about what we will give back to Him in return for His great kindnesses?

The following year the Lord gave Hannah a son, who became one of the greatest prophets of Israel. "And [she] called his name Samuel, saying, 'Because I have asked for him from the Lord'" (1 Samuel 1:20). The first part of Samuel's name is derived from the Hebrew word *shaul*, which means "to ask or petition." The second part of his name—*el*—is the Hebrew word for God. Thus, *Samu-el* means "to ask or petition God."

When the baby had been weaned, Hannah did not go back on her word. She did not play games with God. She took Samuel, the desire of her heart, to the house of the Lord and gave him to Eli, the priest. Once God became first in her heart, the floodgate of blessings opened wide. "And the LORD visited Hannah, so that she conceived and bore three sons and two daughters" (1 Samuel 2:21a).

Why did God allow the woman who was trying to rescue her village to go through so much in order to attain the help she needed? Why did she have to press through enemy territory and then humble herself by begging for help? Why did she have to make a vow of loyalty and faithfulness in order for the elders to come to her rescue? Could it be that God had already given her the victory but was using the circumstances to write an important message on her heart—and on yours as well?

The Lord is saying, *The thing that you desire the most, the thing you are trying to protect, the thing you are holding on to with all of your strength, the thing that you would fight and die for—it must be completely released unto Me. If you are afraid to release that which you cherish and desire the most, you will eventually lose it or you will lose the joy that you hoped it would bring.*

Let me be perfectly clear when I say there is nothing you have that can benefit God. The psalmist wrote, "What shall I render to the LORD For all His benefits toward me?" (Psalm 116:12). No amount of silver, gold, or earthly possessions would ever be enough for you to move Him into action, for He owns the cattle on a thousand hills. So what does God want from you that will cause Him to act on your behalf? The answer is very simple: *you.*

God wants you to trust Him with your life and everything that is in your life. No more fears, no more doubts, and no more anxieties—just complete reliance on the one that holds your life in His hands. God will not possess you against your will. You must surrender your life to Him freely and completely. When your heart becomes one with His heart and your desires one with His desires, He will not hesitate to grant your full petition.

GOD MAY HONOR YOUR PETITION BY PUTTING YOUR FAITH INTO ACTION

The heroine that set out to save her village began the journey with a heartfelt request for the Lord's help. Little did she know that God would require her to extend all the human effort she could muster in order to reach her desired end. Yes, she prayed, and yes, God heard her cry. Yet the Lord did not choose to perform the kind of miracle that would allow the woman to "sit pretty" while He did all the work.

The Lord had a better idea. The woman would be His companion in the deliverance of her people. What better way to build her leadership skills, her character, her faith, her endurance? What a marvelous design for causing her to die to a limited self-image and become fully alive to her God-image and to His plan for her life!

For some, sitting on the sidelines with a full view of a miracle in progress is more than enough excitement for one day. But the Lord has designed some of us with an appetite for challenge and adventure. When Jesus was crucified, His male disciples went into hiding for fear they would face the same terrible fate. Only a woman, Mary Magdalene, ignored the threat of Roman soldiers and went to the tomb where Jesus was buried. This same woman was the first to speak to Jesus and the first to proclaim to the fearful disciples that the Savior had risen from the dead.

In another Bible story, there was a certain widow that came to the prophet Elisha begging for help when her creditors threatened to sell her sons into slavery? The Lord could have honored her petition by causing the money she needed to miraculously appear. Instead He put her faith to work in a very practical way: He introduced the widow and her two sons to the oil business. "So Elisha said to her, 'What shall I do for you? Tell me, what do you have in the house?' And she said, 'Your maidservant has nothing in the house but a jar of oil'" (2 Kings 4:2).

The prophet instructed the widow to borrow as many empty vessels as she could from her neighbors, then to shut the door (to prevent anyone from seeing the miracle that God was going to work). When the woman and her sons began to distribute the single jar of oil among the empty vessels, they discovered that they possessed enough to fill every available vessel. The prophet then instructed the woman to sell the oil and pay her debts.

The Lord not only honored the widow's petition, He also revealed that she didn't have to accept financial ruin. In the midst of a crisis, God handled the immediate concern and developed the woman's business skills—skills that she and her sons probably made use of for the rest of their lives. The widow received an enormous payback for putting her faith to work in obedience to God!

God Reads the Petitions of the Heart

Perhaps the determined heroine in our opening story did not realize that her very appearance before the elders spoke volumes. She and her baby were exhausted, but she had somehow managed to complete the treacherous journey. They asked questions and challenged her petition, but even if she had not spoken a single word, it still would have been evident that her need was very great. You have probably asked yourself at one time or another, *Does God acknowledge the petition of my heart whether it is spoken or unspoken?* The answer to that question is answered in 2 Kings chapter 4.

There is a nameless woman in the Old Testament that is only known as "a notable woman" (2 Kings 4:8). She stands in stark contrast to the weeping image of Hannah, who was drunk with sorrow. Thoughts of personal desire did not distract this woman; rather, she was a woman of deep spiritual contentment.

She also possessed the gift of hospitality. Her thoughts were on the prophet Elisha and his need for a comfortable place to rest as he frequently traveled by on the road near her house. With her husband's permission she built a special guest room onto their house just for Elisha. The prophet was so grateful that he wanted to repay the woman's kindness. He offered to present her to the king, but she wasn't interested in social status. It was clear that the Shunammite woman was perfectly content with caring for her husband and serving the prophet.

But Elisha was determined to repay her kindness and hospitality. He consulted with his servant Gehazi: "'What then is to be done for her?' And Gehazi answered, 'Actually, she has no son, and her husband is old'" (2 Kings 4:14).

Much like Hannah, this notable woman bore the mark of barrenness. She endured social disgrace in her community. But unlike Hannah, she never complained or attempted to use her relationship with the prophet Elisha to help her fulfill the void in her life. Instead of focusing on what she needed from God, she focused on how to faithfully serve the Lord. Through Elisha, the Lord answered this woman's secret petition. One year after she added a new room onto her house for the prophet, she joyfully made room for her new son.

What lesson can you learn from this "notable woman"? No matter how desperate your need, don't allow delays or the passage of time to make you think that God does not acknowledge the desires of your heart. It is when life seems barren and unfulfilling that God teaches you to let go of feelings that create stress and anxiety. Finally, learn to rest in Him: "Rest in the LORD, and wait patiently for Him" (Psalm 37:7a).

Try to think of delays, confusion, and rejection as exercise equipment that God uses to build your faith. "And not only that, but we also glory in tribulations, knowing that tribulation produces perseverance; and perseverance, character; and character, hope" (Romans 5:3–4).

In a final word concerning your petitions to the Lord, let me add that petitions travel best on the wings of praise. A song of praise in the midst of distress not only calms your fears, it reminds you of the power and faithfulness of the Lord. Praise demonstrates to the Lord that your dependence rests solely upon Him.

When King Jehoshaphat was faced with an invading army, he sealed his petition in an envelope of praise:

Now when they began to sing and to praise, the LORD set ambushes against the people of Ammon, Moab, and Mount Seir, who had come against Judah; and they were defeated. (2 Chronicles 20:22)

The Lord will always hear the petitions of your heart. The woman who could not pay her debts, Hannah, and the "notable woman" all learned that He is worthy of our complete trust. My prayer is that God will give you the grace to accept the simplicity or uniqueness of His divine answers—and that you will then discover the powerful things that only a woman can do.

CHAPTER SEVEN

Celebrating the Victory

The woman waited nervously in the neighboring village, wondering if the soldiers would successfully drive out her enemies. When they returned with news of victory, joy and sorrow flooded her heart. The village was saved—but her husband was lost. The woman thanked the elders and the soldiers from the bottom of her heart, then she and her baby headed back to their home. Her mind would not allow her to imagine life without her husband. She found a peaceful escape by turning her thoughts to her people and the pleasure they were feeling after being delivered from their adversaries.

Nothing could have prepared her for what she encountered when she passed through the village gate. As far as her eyes could see, people lined the road shouting her praises. "Our heroine has come home! She has brought victory to her people!"

The woman's eyes widened in amazement and then grew wet with tears. A thousand questions raced through her mind as the crowd continued to cheer. *What have I done? Why are they thanking me? It was God who saved our village…not me! If the Lord had not sent help, we would have all perished.*

Without a doubt the people were grateful to God, but how

could they not honor the brave woman who stood frozen in her tracks? She stood locked in a state of confusion and wonderment until one of the women took her in her arms and whispered, "Accept what God has done through you and rejoice with us."

This housewife, mother, and neighbor who had suddenly become the heroine of her people fell to her knees. The wings of her spirit fluttered within her and her entire being took flight in praise. Like the women of the Bible—Deborah, Miriam, Hannah, Elizabeth, and Mary—her voice rang out with song:

> Our great and mighty God has shown His awesome, won-
>   drous ways.
> He turned my weakness into strength. Turned my sorrow
>   into praise.

Just as it is important to know how to achieve the victory, it is also important to know how to celebrate.

SING A SONG OF VICTORY

Now is the time for you to sing a song of victory.

What? Do I hear you saying you have no victory to sing about, and therefore no reason to praise God? Let me share with you a well-kept secret: If you learn how to praise the Lord for the small victories, you will also praise Him for the big ones.

I know, sometimes the outcome you desire is so far out of your reach that it seems almost unattainable. I feel that way about running. If I set a goal to run one mile, I don't imagine what the end of a mile looks like. Instead I set shorter goals. I concentrate on running from one tree to the next. Then I set a goal of reaching a large rock that sits by the side of the road. I go on and on, not thinking about the final goal, just the small ones in between.

That is how you need to approach victories. Don't sit around thinking of how you will praise God when He gives you the victory. Praise Him for each small achievement along the way. Remember, these small celebrations are taking you closer to your final victory. Praising the Lord for the smallest victories can bring joy into an otherwise dreary circumstance. Learn to thank God even for the setbacks and the lessons you learn in the process. Remember that the Scriptures say, "In everything give thanks."

Praise, you see, is the compass that guides us to victory. Elizabeth, the mother of John the Baptist, had not yet given birth, but she was pregnant with the promise of the Lord. When her cousin Mary (who was also pregnant—with the promise of Jesus) paid her a visit, Elizabeth spoke these words: "Blessed is she who believed, for there will be a fulfillment of those things which were told her from the Lord" (Luke 1:45).

Even though Mary and Elizabeth had not yet seen the promise, they were both filled with praise. If you are expecting the Lord to give you the victory in your situation, then you must become pregnant with His promise. Remember that God "gives life to the dead and calls those things which do not exist as though they did" (Romans 4:17). You do this by filling your heart and mouth with praise.

Paul and Silas were beaten and thrown into prison, but in the midnight hour they began to praise the Lord as though He had already released them. The virgin Mary was not in a prison cell; rather, she was a prisoner of circumstance. The people around her made ugly accusations about the child she was carrying. Even Joseph, her future husband, thought she had been unfaithful. But the Lord filled her heart with joy when He revealed to her the great gift that would come through her and transform the entire world. In the midst of her life being turned upside-down, she sang a song of praise:

My soul magnifies the Lord,
    And my spirit has rejoiced in God my Savior.
For He has regarded the lowly state of His maidservant;
    For behold, henceforth all generations will call me blessed.
For He who is mighty has done great things for me,
    And holy is His name. (Luke 1:46–49)

Mary had not yet seen the "great things," but she believed they would come to pass. What looked like confusion was really a blessing in disguise.

My heavenly Father has given me many victories. I often recount them when I'm faced with new difficulties. I love to thank Him in advance for triumphs that haven't yet transpired. The following is an excellent example of God's blessing.

Several years ago I was traveling by car on a cross-country trip from Virginia to Los Angeles. My youngest daughter and my nephew were traveling with me. The sun was setting as I headed down the long stretch of deserted highway. A road sign told us we were fifty miles from the town of Midland, Texas.

Suddenly a piece of ruptured truck tire appeared on the highway. Before I could hit the brakes, my car ran over the tire. It felt like I'd hit a piece of concrete. The front hood buckled and it sounded like the engine was crumbling from the impact. Smoke filled the air as the car began losing power.

Looking around, I could see that I was in the middle of nowhere. To make matters worse, darkness was falling. In those days there were no cell phones and I was nowhere near an emergency highway phone. The eyes of my daughter and my nephew were wide with fear.

The steam from my car radiator continued to hiss as the engine made a choking sound and finally died. I tried not to panic. I closed my eyes, took a deep breath, and began to speak out loud: "In the name of Jesus, I have the victory! Satan, you are defeated!"

Over and over, I whispered the name of Jesus. After stirring up my faith, I took another deep breath and tried to start the engine. To my amazement the engine started even though it sounded like rocks bouncing around inside of a washing machine. I pulled onto the highway and began to sing as loud as I could over the noise of the engine: "In the name of Jesus…In the name of Jesus, we have the victory…" Pretty soon two frightened teenagers began to sing along with me: "In the name of Jesus…in the name of Jesus, we have the victory."

The speedometer wouldn't move past twenty-five miles an hour, but my heart was happy just to be limping down the highway. The more the car jerked and the engine choked, the louder we sang. We traveled fifty miles in the dark in a car with an engine that (we later discovered) was completely destroyed.

"How did you get here?" The mechanic asked the following morning. "This car is totaled!" He shook his head as he looked at the crumpled engine.

"The Lord did it," I said, smiling.

"I sure can't fix your car!" he said, frowning. "How are you going to get out of here?"

"I don't know," I answered.

What happened next taught me that the best thing to do in the midst of disaster is to praise God for the victory.

"I'm going to give you a car." The mechanic spoke the words slowly, still shaking his head as though he couldn't believe what he was saying. "When you get back home, call me and we'll work out the payment arrangements."

I am neither exaggerating nor embellishing when I tell you that the mechanic handed me the pink slip to a Ford that was in excellent condition. We continued our trip to California, still singing praises to the Lord. Now when I am faced with a seemingly impossible situation, I think about my little adventure in Midland, Texas, and immediately open my mouth in a song of praise.

From time to time I receive phone calls from troubled friends or family members. I used to pour out a lot of positive words, say a prayer, then read a few Scriptures. But on certain occasions the Lord leads me to minister to people in a different way. Sometimes as I listen to people pour out their hearts, I don't reply with words of comfort or affirmation; I simply sing a song of praise to the Lord. I thank Him for His faithfulness and for the victory.

I remember when a dear friend was very ill with cancer. I went to visit her in the hospital and found her in tremendous pain. Fear was written across her face. I tried to think of what Scriptures to read. I tried to think of words of encouragement. But all I could do was look into the eyes of my dear friend who was suffering. When I opened my mouth, the song "Great Is Thy Faithfulness" came from my lips. My friend smiled as she closed her eyes; she even tried to sing the words with me as I continued to praise the Lord.

I have no delusions about being a great singer. And that's okay, because musical ability has nothing to do with an offering of praise. Songs of praise do not emanate from the vocal chords; they come from the deepest recesses of the heart.

When the Lord gives you the victory, there is no better way to give thanks than to offer a heartfelt song of praise.

> Therefore do not be unwise, but understand what the will of the Lord is.… Be filled with the Spirit, speaking to one another in psalms and hymns and spiritual songs, singing and making melody in your heart to the Lord. (Ephesians 5:17–19)

To make melody in your heart is not only to give praise to the Lord, it is to rehearse the blessings of the Lord. It is important to sing praises to the Lord because music has the power to open the chambers of your mind and lock in the precious memories of great blessings and great victories.

I bet you can still remember the songs you used to sing when you were a child. You memorized the alphabet to music and your first introduction to the Scriptures probably came by way of a song. "Jesus loves me, this I know, for the Bible tells me so." When the Lord does great things in your life, a song of praise helps you to remember the victory. Without a doubt, the enemy will come to challenge you again. If you lose the memory of previous victories, you will find yourself doubting God's power to deliver you anew.

That is why the Lord has given us songs of praise that are more memorable than the national anthem. Think about songs with words like "To God be the glory, great things He has done." Those very words were designed to jar your memory with thoughts of what the Lord has accomplished for individuals and nations. There are private victories that you may never be able to share with others, but no one can judge you when you lift your voice to the Lord and thank Him for personal blessings with all your heart and soul.

There will be other times, however, when your testimony of victory will be the weapon used by the Lord to encourage someone who feels defeated and discouraged. As you share what the Lord has done for you, it's like a song in your heart that will stir up waves of thanksgiving and inspire faith in others.

Each morning you should try this simple exercise. Find a quiet place such as your car, bedroom, or a nearby park. Think about something wonderful that the Lord has done in your life. It may have happened yesterday, last year, or ten years ago. It doesn't matter when or where—your assignment is to rehearse the victories. Recount the situation, the fear that was turned to faith, and the ways the Lord moved on your behalf. Give thanks for all of God's blessings.

I want to further recommend that you read through the Bible

and find Scriptures that fit your victorious situation. Write a brief testimony, then write the Scripture next to it. Sing or read the Scripture out loud. The following are examples that you can follow:

Deliverance from Strife—Family/Friends/School/Workplace

Evening and morning and at noon I will pray, and cry aloud,
> And He shall hear my voice.
He has redeemed my soul in peace from the battle which was against me,
> For there were many against me. (Psalm 55:17–18)

Why are you cast down, O my soul?
> And why are you disquieted within me?
Hope in God, for I shall yet praise Him
> For the help of His countenance. (Psalm 42:5)

Praise for Deliverance in Legal Matters

But I will sing of Your power;
> Yes, I will sing aloud of Your mercy in the morning;
For You have been my defense
> And refuge in the day of my trouble. (Psalm 59:16)

Praise for Love and Marriage

He brought me to the banqueting house,
> And his banner over me was love....
Set me as a seal upon your heart,
> As a seal upon your arm;
For love is as strong as death....
> Many waters cannot quench love,
Nor can the floods drown it.
> If a man would give for love

All the wealth of his house,
It would be utterly despised. (Song of Solomon 2:4; 8:6–7)

Praise for Having Children

Praise the LORD!
Praise, O servants of the LORD,
Praise the name of the LORD!…
He grants the barren woman a home,
Like a joyful mother of children.
Praise the LORD! (Psalm 113:1, 9)

Praise for Saving Children

He will save the children of the needy,
And will break in pieces the oppressor. (Psalm 72:4b)

Praise for Healing

O LORD my God, I cried out to You,
And You healed me.
O LORD, You brought my soul up from the grave;
You have kept me alive, that I should not go down
to the pit.
Sing praise to the LORD, You saints of His,
And give thanks at the remembrance of His holy name.
(Psalm 30:2–4)

Praise for Finances

Blessed is the man who fears the LORD,
Who delights greatly in His commandments.
Wealth and riches will be in his house. (Psalm 112:1, 3)

You, O God, sent a plentiful rain,
Whereby You confirmed Your inheritance.…

You, O God, provided from Your goodness for the poor.
(Psalm 68:9–10)

Praise for Deliverance from Enemies

He sent from above, He took me;
>   He drew me out of many waters.
He delivered me from my strong enemy,
>   From those who hated me,
For they were too strong for me....
>   He delivered me because He delighted in me. (Psalm
18:16–17, 19b)

Praise for Deliverance from Depression

I waited patiently for the LORD;
>   And He inclined to me,
And heard my cry.
>   He also brought me up out of a horrible pit,
Out of the miry clay,
>   And set my feet upon a rock,
And established my steps.
>   He has put a new song in my mouth—
Praise to our God;
>   Many will see it and fear,
And will trust in the LORD. (Psalm 40:1–3)

Praise for Deliverance from Hurt

The LORD is near to those who have a broken heart,
>   And saves such as have a contrite spirit.
Many are the afflictions of the righteous,
>   But the LORD delivers him out of them all. (Psalm
34:18–19)

Praise for Deliverance from Fear

> The LORD is my light and my salvation;
>> Whom shall I fear?
> The LORD is the strength of my life;
>> Of whom shall I be afraid? (Psalm 27:1)

Always give thanks for the victories in your life. If you have not yet seen the victory, continue to rejoice! I say this with boldness because the Word of God says that you are in a "fixed fight" with the enemy. God has already "stacked the deck" and there's no way for you to lose:

> Now thanks be to God who always leads us in triumph in Christ, and through us diffuses the fragrance of His knowledge in every place. (2 Corinthians 2:14)

WALKING IN VICTORY

In our opening story, it was at first difficult for the woman to celebrate what the Lord had accomplished through her. She felt that she was not so unique that God would put all the affairs of heaven on hold and come to her aid, make her a heroine, and give her the victory. "Why me?" the woman whispered to herself.

God whispered back, *Why not you?*

Even in the midst of your victory, the demons of insecurity and unworthiness will be there to taunt you and whisper demonic lies: "You don't deserve to be blessed. You're a nobody. You may have the victory now, but it's not going to last. You're a loser!"

My beloved friend, please know that Satan never gives up on you, not even when you have attained the victory. But rejoice, because neither does the Lord give up on you, even when you become fearful about walking in victory. The Lord knows the enemy will attempt to sabotage your triumph.

The Lord also knows that when you've been facing trouble, experiencing hurt, or feeling bound by sin for an extended period of time, you can become comfortable in your miserable state. When God changes your life and gives you peace, joy, provision, love, and success, it can feel so uncomfortable and so unfamiliar that the devil points you to the self-destruct button. Satan tries to get you to push the button so your life can get back to normal—the familiar routine of being in a big mess. Thankfully, the Holy Spirit is there to comfort you and to teach you how to accept and live in the daily routine of peace, joy, fruitfulness, and love as God's child, loved and accepted.

If the Lord heals you from a serious illness, He doesn't want you walking around in fear, wondering if you're going to get sick again. For years I suffered with back trouble. I was hospitalized many times. My mind was in a perpetual fog from the effect of pain pills and muscle relaxants. One Sunday night during a church service the Lord supernaturally healed my back. I was praying for a friend and suddenly, the pain left my back. For weeks I waited for the pain to return. Each day I looked at my medications and wondered when I would have to take them again. I think the Lord must've gotten fed up with my doubt, because He decided to let me know that I was really healed.

One morning as I was walking downstairs, I lost my footing and fell flat on my lower back. I lay there picturing myself in a hospital bed wearing a collar and a back brace. Then I felt the Holy Spirit whisper, *Get up—you're fine!* Slowly I rose to my feet, waiting for the pain to return. To my amazement, I was fine. I heard the Lord say: *Now do you believe Me?*

There will be times when the Lord rescues you from sinful behavior or a fearful situation. Deep inside you may think you are the same terrible person, and that if faced with the same situation, you would fall into your old behavior. You know what God does?

He allows you to confront the behavior He gave you the victory over so that you will know, beyond the shadow of a doubt, the power of God's saving grace.

Here are some ways to continue walking in victory.

Don't Allow the Devil to Tell You That You Are Not Worthy

Let the devil know that you agree with him. None of us are worthy. No matter how good you've been or how perfect you act, we are all sinners saved by the grace of God. One songwriter summed it up this way: "Amazing Grace! How sweet the sound, that saved a wretch like me." The composer of this song, John Newton, was a slave trader that did evil in the sight of the Lord. But when he became a Christian, he repented of his evil deeds.[1]

No one knows better than us what we are really like on the inside, of the evil that we are capable of committing. Without the saving grace of Jesus, thoughts of evil deeds are like millstones around our necks, drowning us in feelings of shame and unworthiness.

Christ saves you from the person you had become and transforms you into the person He wants you to be. If you are twisted, He can straighten you out; if you are in bondage, He can set you free; if you are physically or emotionally ill, He can heal you; if you are lost, He can help you find your way.

So when the devil tells you that you are not worthy of the victory God has given, put a big smile on your face and agree with your adversary. Then lift your hands and praise God for His compassion, His grace, His mercy, and His love. Decide that you will live your life with humility and complete dependence upon the Lord. Remind yourself—in a positive, not a condemning, way—that in spite of your victory, you are just a sinner saved by grace and made worthy because you are now a child of the Most High God.

There are no greater candidates for failure than women who

believe victory comes as a result of righteousness or human effort. When we center on what "we" accomplished because "we" are so great, talented, diligent, or brilliant, we are asking for a fall. The Scriptures tell us, "Pride goes before destruction, / And a haughty spirit before a fall" (Proverbs 16:18).

Bless Those Who Struggle with You; Forgive the Others

After you cross the finish line of struggle and wave the flag of victory, there will be time to focus on the people around you. When you look into the eyes of those who helped you and believed in you, you will feel unspeakable joy and will have ties of love and trust that can never be broken. Support from a husband or wife during a crisis can strengthen a marriage; family and friends that were there for you become the stabilizing force that will help you face the future. There is nothing more satisfying than the opportunity to bless those who have been a blessing in your life.

You will also recall the nameless people (perhaps angels in disguise) who were led by the Lord to help and bless you along the way. The kindness of strangers will remind you to be compassionate to anyone who may need your assistance in a time of difficulty.

But what about the people who were critical, who refused to support your efforts? What about the ones who laughed, gossiped, and even openly attempted to hinder you? Even more painful is the thought of those people who were completely indifferent to your struggle. They didn't care whether you lived or died.

Please listen to me carefully. You may be bitter and hurt because of what someone did to you. Friends or family members may have turned their backs on you in your time of need. Now that God has given you the victory, those same people applaud you, congratulate you, maybe even offer their support and assistance. Please don't let resentment make you a prisoner of hate all over again. Release those who abandoned you, betrayed you, or rejected you.

If God has the power to bring you through a difficult situation, then know that He also has the power to help you forgive. When the people who hurt you ask for forgiveness or offer their friendship, the Lord will give you the same grace He extended when *you* needed forgiveness. The more the Lord heals your emotions, the more you can walk in love and forgiveness with those who have hurt you. Scripture gives us clear direction on this: "Be kind and compassionate to one another, forgiving each other, just as in Christ God forgave you" (Ephesians 4:32, NIV).

Imagine how Peter must have felt after betraying Jesus. Yet after His victorious resurrection Jesus sent for Peter, forgave him, and set him over the church. How humbling for Peter to know that after he had betrayed his dear friend, Jesus had the grace not only to forgive, but to bless Peter. After Peter was given a second chance, he proved to be a faithful friend for the rest of his life.

Sometimes what those people need most is a second chance. It doesn't guarantee that they won't blow it again, but at least you have the ability to stand in the presence of God free from hate and bitterness. When your heart is not blocked by unforgiveness, it becomes an open vessel into which the Lord can pour new and exciting blessings.

You Are Now a Double Threat to Satan's Kingdom

When the Lord brings you through a difficult time and you experience victory, you will have learned a very important lesson: In the most difficult of circumstances, your adversary—no matter how great—can be defeated. You have also learned that reliance on God is the key to victory.

While the ink is still wet on your diploma from spiritual warfare school, the devil calls an emergency meeting in the boardroom of hell. I can almost hear the demons crying out to their master, "What if this victorious Christian is so filled with confidence in God and the power of His authority that she decides to make war on our kingdom? What if she can no longer be intimidated by us and blocks our attacks against others?"

The devil smiles, then roars back, "Remember this! She's *only a woman!* She will pray and ask her Lord to bless her with a wonderful marriage, a pretty house, and nice little children. Of course He will oblige, because after all, she's been through so much and remained so faithful."

A snarling demon replies, "But won't that make her love her God even more and do His will even more?"

The devil's laughter is almost hysterical with pleasure. "Don't you see? The woman will be so happy with her little family that she won't have time for God. She'll be too busy giving parties, helping her husband, and taking her kids to McDonald's for Happy Meals. Ha, ha, ha!"

A slimy demon bobs his head up and down. "Yeah, I see it all the time. Give a woman a few trinkets to play with and she's out of the game. She's no threat to our kingdom—she's *only a woman!*"

Such conversations from Satan's kingdom are why you can't afford to live in a dream world called "happily ever after." The Lord will give you the victory, but the challenges will continue to come. The Lord doesn't isolate you from the conflicts of life; rather, He uses them to keep you focused and dependent upon Him. The challenges force you to grow and mature into the woman He called you to be from your mother's womb—a woman who is wise and has notches on her belt when it comes to spiritual warfare.

Please don't think you're too young to be filled with wisdom and understanding. One of the most powerful weapons in the hand of God is a young woman who dedicates her life to being used by the Lord. Notice in the Bible that the Lord used many people while they were young. Daniel was young when he was taken captive. David was young when he killed the giant. Esther was young when she saved her people. The list goes on and on. One young psalmist wrote:

> You, through Your commandments, make me wiser than
> my enemies;
>> For they are ever with me.
> I have more understanding than all my teachers,
>> For Your testimonies are my meditation.
> I understand more than the ancients,
>> Because I keep Your precepts. (Psalm 119:98–100)

If you are young you are in the perfect position to learn about spiritual warfare, because young women in their teens and early twenties are a high priority target for the devil. Satan will use drugs, sex, ungodly friendships, and rebellion to destroy your life at an early age. But if you develop a strong prayer life and dedicate yourself to learning the Word of God, the Lord will make your way prosperous, and you will have success.

Does serving God mean that a woman should not focus on education, a career, marriage, building a family, or raising children? Nothing could be further from the truth. I am only repeating what the Word of God tells us:

> And whatever you do, do it heartily, as to the Lord and not
> to men, knowing that from the Lord you will receive the
> reward of the inheritance; for you serve the Lord Christ.
> (Colossians 3:23–24)

If you are going to school, ask the Lord to show you how to use the knowledge you are acquiring to glorify God, to destroy the works of Satan, and to build God's kingdom. If you have a career, focus on making it a ministry. Use your influence and resources to help your community and to build the kingdom of God here on earth. If you hope to marry, ask God to bring you a spouse that desires to serve the Lord and to raise a family that brings glory to Him. If you are already married, pray daily with your marriage partner. Ask for God's direction about how you can serve Him as a couple. If you have children, raise them to love God and obey His commandments.

Believe me when I tell you that if you implement these strategies there will be another emergency boardroom meeting in hell. The demons will cry out, "But I thought you said she was *'only a woman!'*"

Satan will frown and snarl. "I know what I said, but there are certain women we must keep an eye on. Like Esther and Deborah before her, she has discovered her strength in God and she knows there are some things that only a woman can do!"

PART TWO

THE STORY OF
A NEW WOMAN

*W*as it a dream or was she wide awake? The woman never imagined that caring for a child alone would be like swimming against a swift current in uncharted waters. She had imagined that her life would be peaceful once the struggle in her village had ended. Instead she found herself facing a new and invisible adversary who was trying to invade her heart and soul. If this dark foe called loneliness succeeded in gaining control, she would be ruled by an enemy more terrifying than the one that had attempted to destroy her village.

In public gatherings, the woman seemed confident and secure. After all, she had taken on the enemy and prevailed. How could the people around her imagine the private war of fear and loneliness that was raging within her mind, body, and soul? Her head constantly ached from the fear of not having enough money to live on. The people in her village were loving and supportive, but they had their own families to care for. What if one day they couldn't help her anymore? How could she make a living and support her child?

Other matters also plagued her mind. At one time her only concern had been taking care of her husband and baby; now, after her rite of passage through the forest, that way of life had been forever altered. She wanted to help her village become strong and productive again, but she was afraid of what the people would think if she dared to meddle in the affairs of the elders. Her fears made her want to forget about her new ideas, but the ideas refused to die.

Her vision was to bring all the neighboring villages together to form a joint council. But how could she go about making the elders see the need? If she could convince them, the villages could work out an agreement to stand together in the event of another enemy attack.

When the woman could no longer contain her thoughts, she swallowed her fears and spoke to the elders. Unfortunately, they were less than receptive. The leader of the elders was the first to speak: "You have enough concerns taking care of yourself and a young child. Let the men worry about such weighty matters."

Another elder smiled at her. "It was terrible that you had to endure such hardships to help our people. But rest assured that we are here to protect you and to see that you are never burdened with such a great responsibility again."

"Yes," a third elder agreed. "It is our duty before God not to depend upon, but to defend, the weaker members of our village; after all, you're only—"

The woman raised her hand. "I know what I am. And I know what God is telling me. Say what you like and do as you choose, but the day will come when you will need me again."

She looked at them with fire in her eyes. One by one the elders dropped their heads. When she felt the tears stinging her eyes, she turned and walked out.

The heaviness of their rejection pressed against her soul as she walked back to her house. "Lord, is this my reward for obeying your voice—to live in this world unwanted and alone?"

As the days passed the woman came to dread what had once been her favorite pastime: gathering for conversation with her women friends and neighbors. Each time she tried to raise the subject of replanting the crops that had been ruined by the invading army or of rebuilding the houses that had been burned, the women who had once delighted in her company looked at her as though she were speaking a different language.

"The men will take care of such matters!" an elder's wife said. Then she returned to her conversation about her husband and children.

The woman's heart ached as she listened to them talk about their families and their comfortable lives. No matter how hard she tried, she didn't seem to fit in anywhere. The reality of her new life was like waking from a nightmare only to find that she was better off asleep.

There were times when the grief of losing her husband was almost unbearable. A close friend tried to comfort her: "Don't worry, you'll marry again. Then your life will be happy."

The woman tried to find reassurance in her friend's words, but a voice inside told her that her desires would never again be the same and that she needed more than a husband to fill the longing in her heart.

One bright Sunday morning many months later, as she looked up at the sky while walking to church, she became aware of the fact that her time of grieving was over. It was like waking from a deep sleep; now she was prepared to live. Perhaps it was the absence of sadness that lent a brightness to her eyes as she made her way into the small church and chose a seat. She was shining like a gold coin that had just been swept out of a dark corner.

From time to time, some of the older men would stop by the woman's house when they were not busy. They would help her with the work that was made for a man. Some of the husbands would bring her meat and vegetables, but their wives had warned them not to linger and not to drop in too often.

One of the village leaders felt that the wives were being overly cautious. He decided he would help the woman in his spare time. He fixed the locks on her doors and windows. He plowed up a section of ground so that she could expand her garden. He came to love this brave woman as a man loves his sister or his mother.

Summer turned to autumn, and soon a chill could be felt in the air. One day, rain began to pound the earth with the force of heavy stones. The woman grew desperate: Not only was she locked inside by the storms, but the rain itself was forcing its way into her house like a common thief. She tried to stuff rags into the cracks between the doors and windows and to nail pieces of wood over the holes in the ceiling, but it was a losing battle. All she could do was cover her face and weep as the water rushed in through every opening.

Was this the same woman who had made her way through the enemy-infested forest and persuaded the elders of the neighboring village to send their army to help her people? Why was such a small matter paralyzing her mind with fear? As she stood frozen in the middle of the room, biting her lip to keep from screaming, there came a frantic knock at her door.

"Open up before I drown!" It was the voice of the neighbor who had helped her so many times before. Though they rarely exchanged more than a few words anymore, she knew his voice well.

"Should I build you a boat or try to fix these leaks?" The man looked up at the ceiling and smiled. The woman did not answer; she simply lifted her eyes and gazed at the water pouring through the cracks.

It was late evening by the time the man had finished repairing the house. Before heading for home, the woman insisted, he should eat a warm meal—after all, it was the least she could do to repay his kindness.

It was at that moment that *good intentions* emerged from the pit of hell and stepped into the woman's house to examine the man's handiwork. "Well done," the demon applauded the man. "And how else can we comfort this poor woman?"

Conviction frantically attempted to raise the alarm in the hearts of the man and the woman, but both thought they were on solid ground. By the time conviction went to reach for the woman to hold her back, it was too late. She had tripped over the man's good intentions and fallen into a deep pit of need.

It's hard to keep a secret buried in the soil of a small village. No one was ever certain as to what had happened between the man and the woman, but it became common knowledge that the man's wife had forbidden him to ever again set foot on the woman's property. The woman gradually withdrew into the solitude of her home, venturing out only on rare occasions.

When the summer returned, men from the neighboring village came to trade their cattle. These transactions were always very festive. There was music, dancing, lots of food, and young men and women hoping to find mates.

The visitors had heard of the brave young widow, and they were curious to see her. But the woman was not in the least bit interested. Only one thing weighed heavily on her heart: She had strayed from the Lord. The loss of His presence in her life was more than she could bear.

It must not be forgotten, however, that she was a woman of great determination. Whatever it took, she would find her way back to God.

Early one morning the woman rose as usual for a time of prayer. To her dismay her prayers were interrupted by a herd of mooing cows traders were bringing into the village. God drew her attention to the window and caused her to look outside.

"Evil is passing through the gate of the village," the Lord whispered to her spirit. Slowly a picture formed in her mind: She saw an image of sick and dying people. The woman blinked and shook her head, trying to rid her mind of the terrible image.

Lord, what does this mean?

These cows carry a deadly disease. The herders know that the meat will kill your people, but they don't care. They are wicked and full of greed.

What can I do?

Save your people!

But how?

By caring.

Caring?

Yes—caring whether they live or die.

The woman wanted to argue. She wanted to tell the Lord that

the people in the village had hurt her deeply and she didn't care if they lived or died. But her love for God caused her to put aside her feelings and surrender to His will. "Give me a plan," she whispered, staring at the cows through her window. "Show me what to do."

The woman's heart pounded as she pinned a flower in her hair and put on a colorful dress. From beneath a loose floorboard in her house she retrieved a small box of money. She whispered softly to the Lord, *This is all the money I have in the world. You are the supplier of my needs and I will obey Your will.*

The people of the village were consumed with curiosity when the reclusive woman appeared on the street and approached the herdsmen, her young son in tow. Because of her legendary status, the men were already aware of her identity.

She forced a pleasant smile and willed a gentle tone to her voice. "I want to purchase a cow. A large cow."

"And what will one small woman do with such a large animal?" asked the herdsman leader, flashing a toothless grin at her.

"It has been more than a year since the village was saved from our enemies. I want to slaughter the cow and prepare a banquet for the elders and their families."

"Because you are a woman of great renown, I will charge you only half the price of the cow." The man bowed respectfully, then extended his hand for the money. The woman obliged, then requested that the men of her village slaughter it for the feast.

The woman bade the herdsmen farewell, then began to walk back to her home. Suddenly she stopped and turned back to the herdsmen. "I do hope you will stay and join us for the celebration," she called to them.

The men looked at one another. "Well…" The leader cleared his throat. "We would love to join you, but it's a long way to the next village and we must leave before night falls."

"Come now, it's not that far." the woman's words were like

honey. "Surely there will be enough time for you to dine at our table and still reach your destination."

The herdsmen stuttered and stammered amongst themselves. Finally one said, "Let us see how the trading goes today. If time permits, perhaps we will be able to sit down for a moment."

"Good," the woman said. "I will ask the Lord to reward your kindness to me by allowing you to dine with us this evening."

The woman was bold in the face of her enemies, but she was shaking all over by the time she reached her home. "Lord, don't let my plan fail! Block the enemies of my people. Don't let them escape."

Suddenly she felt the Lord's voice. *My child, this isn't your plan; it's My plan. These evil men will never escape.*

The words brought comfort to the woman. She raised her hands and began singing a song of praise.

The sun was setting in the sky and the air was thick with the smell of beef roasting over an open fire. The last of the money and goods had changed hands when the village people gathered around the campfire and prepared to feast.

"I have a special place for you at the head of the table," the woman said to the leader of the herdsmen. For a moment the man was taken by surprise. He cleared his throat and tried to smile. "It's terribly late and my men and I must hurry on."

"Please. Just sit with us for a little while. The people will be offended if you refuse our hospitality."

The man nervously took a seat at the head of the table. He picked up a piece of fruit and began to eat, then washed it down with a cup of spring water. The other herdsmen also slowly gathered at the table. Hesitantly, they filled their bowls with vegetables and proceeded to gulp down the food.

The elders were not pleased at how the woman was taking charge of the celebration, and found the familiarity with which she was treating these male visitors a bit disquieting. For months she had been a recluse; now she was flitting about freely. Perhaps the rumors are true, the elders thought to themselves. Maybe she is a woman of questionable character after all.

The woman stood up, smiling broadly at the group of herdsmen. "Dear friends, we cannot allow you to leave without being the first to taste of the meat from the roasted cow. After all, if you had not come to our village this meat would not be here for our people to enjoy."

The lead herdsman stood up from the table. "We have already stayed too long! We must be leaving," he insisted.

"Yes! We must leave immediately!" the other herdsmen echoed.

The woman's heart pounded in fear. She prayed the men would not read the panic in her eyes. "Please do not deprive us of your company. Fill your stomachs with meat so that you won't be hungry on your journey."

"Thank you for your hospitality, but we cannot stay!" the leader said.

No one was prepared for what happened next. A man stepped out of the shadows to face the herdsmen. It was the same man who on a rainy day had brought first comfort, then shame, to the woman. He seemed oblivious to the stares and whispers as he challenged the herdsmen.

"Is there a reason you refuse to eat the meat you sold to our people?" he asked.

"How ridiculous!" the leader protested. "There is nothing wrong with the meat!"

The man glared at the herdsmen. "If the meat is good, you can prove it by eating a piece. But if you refuse to eat, we will know the truth."

The herdsmen trembled as the elders gathered to stand behind the man confronting them. Slowly the leader of the herdsmen reached inside of his coat and brought out his money pouch. He dropped it on the table, then looked at the men that were with him. One by one, each of the men walked to the table and returned the money and goods they had taken from the people.

The people watched as the wicked men turned and disappeared into the shadows that came from the evening sky.

"Slaughter the cattle and bury them in a ditch!" an elder ordered.

Only the man who had came to the woman's defense noticed her walk quietly away. He watched as she pulled the flower from her hair, entered her house, and closed the door firmly behind her. He didn't see her fall on her knees in praise and thanksgiving.

The next day should have seen great celebration; instead, the elders met from sunup to sundown in heated discussion.

"Once again if it had not been for that woman we would all have died," the leader of the elders said. "I say we make her an elder of this village."

"What kind of devil is speaking through you?" another elder protested. "The woman has bewitched you. That must be why you are speaking so foolishly!"

The arguing continued, but in the end the chief elder and two others went to the woman's house. She opened her front door before they knocked; she did not seem the least bit surprised by their presence. The leader spoke first. "We have come to ask forgiveness for doubting you. And…and…"

"And what?" the woman asked.

"And to ask you to become an elder of our village," the man finally said.

Before she could answer, another elder spoke. "It is clear to us that God Himself has already made you an elder to our people. You see with the eyes of the Lord and you always help us in times of trouble. So we are pleading with you to sit in our midst, to share your wisdom, and to give us counsel from God."

The Lord had already prepared the woman for the visit from the men that were standing before her. And she had already told the Lord that she would do whatever was asked of her.

It wasn't easy for many of the villagers to accept a female elder. Some recalled the rumors and felt it was dangerous for her to be put into a position in which she was constantly in the company of men—especially since she had no husband of her own. But despite the concerns and the resistance, no one could deny that the village became a better place once the counsel of the woman became law.

For two years the Lord watched her dedication, her integrity, and her love for the people. Then in the third year the vision the woman carried was finally birthed. All the neighboring villages gathered together to form an alliance and to make a verbal agreement to help one another in times of trouble.

One of the men from a neighboring village was a prominent leader who had recently lost his wife in childbirth. He listened to the woman as she shared her vision with the council of elders. Her speech was gentle and gracious, yet powerful. His heart was deeply moved by her.

He could have used his influence to arrange a marriage between the two of them, but in the woman he saw potential for something much deeper. This woman had a sense of destiny and purpose about her. Somehow she had managed to break free of the complacency that shrouded the people around her.

The man was as wise as he was creative in his thinking. He reasoned that in order to fully experience all that was hiding in the heart of the woman, she would have to be the one to do the choosing.

Long ago, when he had first been celebrated as a brave young warrior, a girl in their village had become the desire of his eyes. Learning of this, his father had taken him for a long walk in the woods and shared with him about the mystery of a woman's heart.

"My son, when a man of power and authority humbles himself and becomes the servant of whatever love demands, his reward is far greater than that of the man who sets himself up as the ruler of love."

He had never forgotten his father's advice. Even now, as he began pursuing this brave woman from the neighboring village, he followed that counsel. He spoke only enough words to draw her eyes to the deeds of his heart. She watched as he committed himself to becoming the servant of her every desire. It was then that she chose to love him.

How much did she love him? Multiply all that you could ever hope to find in the deep caverns of love and count it as one grain of sand when compared to what the woman felt. Her joy was unfathomable. The man's heart was overflowing, because only a woman as special as the woman God had given him could make his life so complete.

They married when the harvest of grain was as full as the harvest of love. He took her son as his own. And so they continued.

CHAPTER EIGHT

The Process of Transformation

he chapters of life continue until we come to the final page. And so it was that after the woman finally received the honor she deserved from the elders and settled down with her new husband, it was not the end of the story, just a beautiful pause—something like the first warm, balmy day of an early spring that is deeply appreciated after a long, cold winter.

I think it is important to revisit the most recent phase of the woman's journey and examine what it took for her to arrive at a place of love and triumph. Please know that with each victory the Lord allows, He is training you and strengthening you for even greater challenges.

When God begins to transform your life, it will take more than a single event. Transformation is a continuous process in which you pass through seasons that are calm and uneventful and seasons that are filled with storms and trials. In the second part of the story, it is clear that the woman went through another season of difficulty before coming to a place of rejoicing.

You probably know by now that on the road of life many important lessons can be learned when we take the time to explore the terrain. One of the important aspects of transformation is the emotional upheaval found in releasing the past and trying to settle into a new life. The woman in our story went through a period of mourning—not only for her husband, but for the life she once lived.

Even when you understand that "all things work together for good to those who love God, to those who are the called according to His purpose" (Romans 8:28), you still have to make adjustments. To help you get through the tough times the Lord created a special medicine called *time and understanding* to heal the hurts of past memories. The more time there is between you and the events of your past, the more you can look back and see why the Lord allowed certain events to take place.

Perhaps you recall that the woman in our story was walking to church one morning and suddenly realized that her grieving had ended. It takes time to understand and find comfort in the sovereign ways of God. But even with time, there are things in life that you will probably never understand until you see God face-to-face.

There is still another view of the losses and disappointments that I want to share with you. A passage in the book of Isaiah says the following: "No weapon formed against you shall prosper" (Isaiah 54:17a). Let me remind you that God loves you and has a perfect plan for your life. Many times the choices you make are choices that, in the long run, will not benefit you and actually work against God's plan. So the Lord makes this wonderful yet sometimes hard-to-deal-with promise that if any type of weapon is formed against you, He will not allow it to prosper.

Perhaps you see an opportunity that appears to be beneficial, yet God knows that in the long run it is a weapon that will work against you. Maybe a relationship suddenly fails or the door marked *Opportunity* slams in your face. It could be that the marriage proposal does not lead to a wedding, or that the "opportunity of a lifetime" fails to prosper.

You may not understand why certain difficulties have transpired, but the Scriptures remind us that no matter how things appear we should rejoice. "In everything give thanks; for this is the will of God in Christ Jesus for you" (1 Thessalonians 5:18). Somewhere along the journey of your transformation, you will hopefully come to understand God's divine intervention and joyfully give thanks.

THE LOVE OF GOD IN ACTION

The process of transformation is not always painful or turbulent. The Scriptures clearly demonstrate that for some people transformation is dramatic, while for others it can happen as quietly as the dawning of a new day.

In Matthew 9:9, Jesus spoke two words to a young man known as Levi the tax collector: "Follow me." And Levi rose and followed Him. There were no earthshaking events, only an offer from Jesus and Levi's resounding yes. Immediately Jesus gave the former tax collector and enemy of the Jewish people a new life, a new occupation, and a new name, Matthew. This faithful disciple went on to do great things for God. The full potential for Matthew's life was realized because he made a simple decision to follow Jesus.

When it comes to transformation, the Lord sometimes orders a divine interruption to set us on a new path. At other times, He uses a powerful yet gentle instrument called love. God's love can gradually and quietly transform us into the people He desires us to become.

His love may not find you in a place of sin like He did with Matthew. Maybe you are not living up to your full potential of productivity. Perhaps you are filled with secret fears and insecurities. You may be just plain complacent. But I promise you that when the Lord breathes His love into your spirit, your fears, doubts, and passivity will be replaced with confidence, energy, and boldness. "For God has not given us a spirit of fear, but of power and of love and of a sound mind" (2 Timothy 1:7).

I have known people who were once shy or timid but who were transformed once they experienced God's love. One young lady found the confidence to start her own business. Another dear friend lost weight and improved her appearance. These things transpired because the love of God made these women feel important and valuable.

But what about the woman who is so deeply entrenched in sin she actually believes it is too late for God to transform her life? Please understand that the devil can blind you—not only to the power of God, but also to His unlimited love and compassion. Even when people give up on you and you, in turn, give up on yourself, God never gives up on His mission to transform your life.

When you become a prisoner of sin, you make mistakes that lead you to a place of guilt and shame. To be covered in shame is like wearing a garment that has a terrible stench. When you are around people, you can tell by the repulsed looks on their faces that they view you as unacceptable. Even if you possess wealth and power, you cannot find peace if you are reeking with the odor of shame.

But the Lord loves you so much that He looks beyond your faults. He sees the needs you are trying so desperately to fill—the needs for love and acceptance. Perhaps you have tried all the wrong things and come close to destroying yourself. I have been in that very place, and I am so glad that the following Scripture found me when I was searching for forgiveness: "He raiseth up the poor out of the dust, and lifteth the needy out of the dunghill" (Psalm 113:7, KJV).

In biblical times, the dunghill was a trash pile of human and animal waste. As you can imagine, the smell was unbearable. I want you to know that the Lord is responsible for the invention of recycling. The Bible tells us that He searches the dunghills looking for those who have been thrown away or are trying to throw their own lives away. If you are in and out of dunghills, I want you to know that God's love is great—He overlooks the stench of your shame to seek you out. His only thought is to rescue you and to transform you with His love.

When you feel convicted, it is like an alarm that has been placed inside of your spirit by the Lord. He loves you so much that He has set up boundaries within yourself—not to hinder you, but to protect you. When you cross over the boundaries, you set off an alarm of conviction within your spirit. The alarm is there to let you know that you are in a danger zone and need to retreat to the safety of God's love.

The accusing siren of sin is so loud that, once it goes off, you can't run away from it or drown it out with drugs, alcohol, or any other dark pursuits. Satan would have you believe that the siren of conviction is designed to condemn you. He wants you to think that you will never find forgiveness, that God will never take you back. But nothing could be further from the truth.

Guilt was designed not to condemn, but to convict—to make you aware of your mistakes so they can be corrected. Once you confess your sins, the Lord is there to help you get back on the right path. He is the only One who knows the code to shut off the siren of conviction. The code for silencing guilt is simple: "If we confess our sins, He is faithful and just to forgive us our sins and to cleanse us from all unrighteousness" (1 John 1:9).

With an abundance of love, God locates you in the dunghill of sin. Then when He hears your confession, He lifts you from the stench, turns off the alarm, cleans you up, and gives you a new life in Christ.

RENEWING YOUR MIND

Now that we have talked about the nature of God's transforming love, I think it is important that we understand the actual steps of transformation. One of the best lessons is found in the book of Romans. The apostle Paul pleads with believers in the following passage:

> Do not be conformed to this world, but be transformed by the renewing of your mind, that you may prove what is that good and acceptable and perfect will of God. (Romans 12:2)

The woman in our story understood the challenge of not conforming. There was a part of her that would have loved to conform—to fit in with the people in her village—but the spirit of transformation would not allow her to return to the way of life she had once known. Even when the elders of her village rejected the vision that God had given her, she could not go back. The woman of the past was dead and buried; in her place stood a transformed woman.

Paul also went through a major transformation. He fully understood that his plea to the the Roman church to be transformed was like asking them to jump into shark-infested waters and try not to be devoured. The citizens of the Roman culture were sexually immoral in ways we cannot imagine. They worshiped many different gods. They practiced astrology and other mystical rituals. Many of them felt Christianity would be another interesting practice to add to the list of spiritual experiences.

Yet there were also people in Rome who were deeply disturbed by the corruption in their culture. They wanted nothing to do with the depraved Roman lifestyle. Christianity represented a way of escape for them and their families.

For the most part, the people of Rome could not understand the error of their ways. They thought their behavior was perfectly normal. Paul, however, could see the destruction that was waiting at the end of the road. The people to whom he was writing did not need a lifestyle adjustment; they needed a complete spiritual transformation.

Things are not much different today. Many Christians have become comfortable with compromise and corruption. Like drifting on an open sea, they don't recognize how far they are from God. A lifestyle adjustment would be like putting a bandage on a cancer. Transformation is still the only hope for survival.

But what does it really mean to be transformed, as opposed to remaining conformed? The word *conform* has two separate meanings in Greek.[1] The first word is *summorphos,* which is the idea of being fashioned in the same form as another. This, however, is not the meaning of the word *conform* as it is used in Romans 12:2. The Greek word in this passage is the word *suschematizo,* which means being alike on the outside, yet transitory, changeable, and unstable on the inside.

The apostle Paul begged the Roman church not to be wishy-washy like the people of the world. Those people frequently changed gods (as a group), engaged in perverted sexual practices (as a group), and changed philosophies on a whim (always as a group). For me, a simpler definition of the word *suschematizo* is choosing to be a part of a group where you find friendship, support, and acceptance while traveling the long road that leads to hell.

This is why Paul pleads with us from the pages of the book of Romans: "Be transformed by the renewing of your minds." Paul knew the lengths that God would go to in order to achieve the necessary transformation. His own experience had been a painful process. Paul, formerly known as Saul, had persecuted the early church and ordered the death and imprisonment of innocent Christians. He literally did not know what hit him when a light came down from heaven and blinded his eyes. He became the live-in guest of a Christian named Ananias while God transformed Saul into Paul.

As we see in Paul's story, anyone is a candidate for transformation. The Lord may be the only one who sees the spiritual potential buried inside. A classic example of this is found in the story of Mary Magdalene.

The Bible tells us little about this faithful woman who served Jesus during His ministry on earth. Scripture details "certain women who had been healed of evil spirits and infirmities—Mary called Magdalene, out of whom had come seven demons" (Luke 8:2). The only thing we know for certain is that Jesus knew His Father's plan for Mary Magdalene. Once she had been set free, Mary became a woman who was used mightily by God and fulfilled her divine destiny. That's what we remember her for to this day. She probably had no idea of the hidden potential that transformation would bring.

The word *transform* is derived from the Greek word *metamorphoo,*[2] which also translates to the English word "metamorphosis." Webster's Dictionary gives the following definitions of the word: "a.) to change into a different form by supernatural means; b.) a striking alteration in the appearance, character, or circumstances."

A few years ago a toy came on the market that was very unusual. It was called a Transformer. Some of the Transformers looked like small automobiles, but if you pushed a certain button, the automobile would unfold and take on the shape of a man. It's hard to imagine that hiding inside a small toy—one that appeared to be a car with wheels, windows, and doors—was the image of a man who was waiting for the right button to be pushed.

Transformation means that what something *was* has no bearing on what it *will become.* Perhaps you can now understand the full impact of the following Scripture: "Therefore, if anyone is in Christ, he is a new creation; old things have passed away; behold, all things have become new" (2 Corinthians 5:17).

THE RESPONSIBILITY OF TRANSFORMATION

You may be asking what your responsibility is concerning transformation. Is it up to you to freely commit yourself to the process of transformation? Or is it up to God to initiate transformation as He did with the apostle Paul? Paul makes a strong appeal in Romans 12:1–2. Here's my paraphrase: "Please don't go through what I went through in order to be transformed. There is a much easier way: Submit yourself to God and allow Him to give you a new mind."

You may think, "I don't really need to be transformed. I'm fine just the way I am. Maybe I could use a little tweaking, but I don't need an entire transformation." Or maybe you're at the opposite end: "I don't want to go through what Paul went through. I've already been through enough. I surrender—give me the steps to transformation."

I hope that's you. I will offer these steps in the next chapter.

CHAPTER NINE

Putting on the New Creation

W hen the woman in our story put on the garment of her new creation and began to walk in her God-image, it caused quite a stir in her village. The men were curious and even a little intimidated by her quiet strength. The women stared blankly, unable to relate to the visionary thinking that came from her renewed mind.

Perhaps you know what it's like to try to live and work around people who have a completely different mind-set. Once you emerge in the newness of Christ, you quickly discover that you have very little in common with people who live by the world's standards. Still, the Lord does not call you to live in isolation but to find common ground so you can be a light to those in darkness.

When you walk in transformation, you are in a spotlight. The people around watch to see if the "new" you is an act that will eventually fade away or if you've undergone a real and permanent change.

As the Lord continues to mature you and bless you, His presence in your life will be undeniable. Eventually people will either come to respect your beliefs or openly ridicule you for your stance. Don't be surprised if you start feeling like one of the persecuted Christians from the book of Acts. Perhaps those who once opposed you will one day want to know more about your new life in Christ.

As I mentioned in the previous chapter, transformation does not happen in a single event but rather in a continual process. In light of this fact, I want to point out three important steps that lead to transformation. First, your mind must be renewed with the knowledge of God. Second, you must put off the garments of sin. And third, you must put on the garments of righteousness.

These steps to transformation are spelled out in the Scriptures. To me they give the feeling of a spiritual makeover. I say "makeover" because the Bible tells us over and over again what to stop doing (put off) and what to start doing (put on). God does not force us into action, but He urges us to exercise self-discipline and spiritual maturity by *putting off* the things that are destructive and *putting on* the things that are productive.

At this very moment you may be saying to yourself, *but what if I'm not strong enough to put off evil behavior? What if I can't control myself?* Believe me when I tell you that the Lord will send you a strong helper, the Holy Spirit. You will have all the help you need as you put off the old and put on the new.

There is a very important Scripture that provides us with assurance:

> Therefore, my beloved…work out your own salvation with fear and trembling; for it is God who works in you both to will and to do for His good pleasure. (Philippians 2:12–13)

Paul explains that with the indwelling presence of the Holy Spirit in your life the Lord works into every part of your being the power to resist Satan and to experience God's joy. Remember, "the joy of the LORD is your strength" (Nehemiah 8:10). When you rejoice in the Lord, He gives you the strength to work out your weaknesses, separate yourself from ungodly practices, and live in a way that brings honor and glory to His name.

As you consistently apply the Word of God to your life, you will slowly but surely find yourself *transformed* for the better.

A SPIRITUAL MAKEOVER

Let's take a look at the Scriptures that lead to a makeover of the inner person:

> But now you yourselves are to put off all these: anger, wrath, malice, blasphemy, filthy language out of your mouth. Do not lie to one another, since you have *put off the old man* with his deeds. (Colossians 3:8–9, emphasis added)

> Put off, concerning your former conduct, the old man which grows corrupt according to the deceitful lusts, and be renewed in the spirit of your mind. (Ephesians 4:22–23)

But how do I put off the old person and put on the new person? The answer is simple: "Therefore, if anyone is in Christ, he is a new creation; old things have passed away; behold, all things have become new." In other words, you first put on Christ by allowing Him to come into your heart.

It is apparent that many longtime church members don't have Jesus in their hearts. I say this because they lack evidence of salvation, the elements of which include love, compassion, joy, peace, and power over Satan. It's tragic but true. There are also people outside the church who may not know about the transforming power that is available through Jesus Christ.

Whether you are a church member or not, if you desire to become a new creation in Christ, it is not difficult to accomplish: In a simple prayer, confess your sins to God and ask Him to give you the power to turn from your old lifestyle. Ask Jesus to forgive you and come into your heart to be the Lord (boss) and Savior of your life. It is important that you follow this prayer up by finding a church or Bible study to help you to grow spiritually.

Now that you have put off sin and put on Jesus Christ, let's continue your spiritual makeover.

> The night is far spent, the day is at hand. Therefore let us cast off the works of darkness, and let us *put on the armor of light*. Let us walk properly, as in the day, not in revelry and drunkenness, not in lewdness and lust, not in strife and envy. But *put on the Lord Jesus Christ*, and make no provision for the flesh, to fulfill its lusts. (Romans 13:12–14, emphasis added)

Please know that once you commit yourself to the Lord Jesus Christ, He illuminates you with a supernatural light. The light exposes every dark area of your life. It also allows you to see into the dark places where Satan plots to destroy you. With the light of Jesus all around you, evil has no place to hide.

Light also allows you to have understanding and revelation because you are no longer "in the dark." You begin to see things for what they really are. You can see the consequences that are connected with dark behavior. Walking in the light of Jesus Christ brings us into the knowledge that leads to a fulfilled life.

> *Put on the new man* who is renewed in knowledge according to the image of Him who created him. (Colossians 3:10, emphasis added)

Knowledge is the aspect of the light of Christ that ushers in understanding. Where there is knowledge and understanding, Satan cannot use the tool of ignorance to bring about your destruction. Just as the knowledge of natural things can take you from ignorance and incompetence to skill and understanding, so it is with spiritual knowledge.

> For the LORD gives wisdom;
>   From His mouth come knowledge and understanding.
> (Proverbs 2:6)

> And I will give you shepherds according to My heart, who will feed you with knowledge and understanding. (Jeremiah 3:15)

I want to take a moment to note the Hebrew word that is used in the Jeremiah passage to convey "understanding." It is the word *sachal.*[1] This word translates as "the understanding, prudence, and wisdom that come from proper teaching." The word also translates to "prosperity" and "success."

I want to add a joyful footnote to the word *sachal* as Jeremiah used it. In the Hebrew grammatical structure of the verb *sachal,* the tense is causative, infinitive, and absolute. In plain English, that means that Jeremiah, in speaking for the Lord, was saying, "I will give you shepherds according to My heart that will feed you with knowledge and cause you to have continual and unfailing understanding and cause you to continually prosper and to have unfailing success."

When you submit yourself to a pastor and teacher who have been sent from God, part of the evidence of your transformation is spiritual understanding and a certain kind of prosperity and success. Without a doubt, if you pray diligently for a good church home, Bible study, or Bible school, you will succeed in the phase of your transformation that is connected to the renewal of your mind.

Unfortunately we live in a society that is quick to label financial gain as the only success that counts. But God's definition of success is having a renewed mind. If your mind has not been renewed, you may experience public success (money and status) but private failure. The knowledge and understanding that comes from God as a part of your transformation lead to much more than a limited success.

The Lord wants you to have an across-the-board triumph in every area of your life. God wants you to be successfully single or successfully married. He wants you to become a successful parent. He wants you to have success in relationships. God wants you to have the kind of success that brings blessings to everything your transformed hands touch—whether it be in your church, job, school, community, or government. The heavens rejoice when you have the kind of success that causes you to excel, overcome, and glorify God in everything you do.

When wisdom enters your heart,
And knowledge is pleasant to your soul,
Discretion will preserve you;
Understanding will keep you,
To deliver you from the way of evil,
From the man who speaks perverse things. (Proverbs 2:10–12)

Knowledge and understanding allow you to discern good from evil. Once you have gone through the process of transformation, you will have learned how to stand apart from the popular views that lead to entrapment and even destruction. The person who speaks "perverse things" will no longer be attractive and alluring because your heart will hunger for better things. Neither perverse advertising nor false religion will be capable of persuading you to sit at a table and eat poisoned meat.

LIFE AS A NEW CREATION

During her transformation, the woman in our story received spiritual knowledge and understanding that allowed her to recognize the deception of the evil herdsmen. Yet she still found herself standing alone against a great number of people who were completely deceived.

The evidence of a transformed life is the capacity to accept the blindness and weakness of others without condemning them. You cannot allow yourself to become frustrated with those who are weak or deceived. Someone once said, "But for the grace of God, there go I." If God had not given you the ability to recognize deception, you too would be one of those walking in darkness.

Being set apart from the crowd for a season is what I call the process of *spiritual metamorphosis*. God will intentionally set you in a cocoon-like place of isolation where He will strengthen you in your spirit by forcing you to press against and break through the walls of cultural and religious traditions.

The most familiar type of natural metamorphosis is the transformation of a caterpillar into a butterfly. The process provides a wonderful parallel to how God changes our lives.

During metamorphosis, the caterpillar uses fine, silk threads to encase itself in a cocoon. Depending on the type of butterfly that is being hatched, the pupa (what the former caterpillar is when it's between the larval stage and the adult stage) can remain in this seemingly dormant state for anywhere from a few weeks to eight months. Deep inside the silky gold tomb, the miracle of transformation is taking place. Once God finishes His handiwork, He motivates the fragile winged creature to push against the walls of the cocoon until the new butterfly breaks out of the shell. It is during this difficult final stage of breaking out that the butterfly gains the strength it will need to fly.

Just like a little kid, I asked God, "Do caterpillars know they will someday become butterflies, or do you surprise them? Do we know what we will really become, or do you like to surprise us?" I think that most of us are amazed at what God can do with both butterflies and people.

Try to imagine what it would be like if you were a fuzzy, slow-moving caterpillar, inching your way through life. Sometimes you catch glimpses of beautiful butterflies fluttering about, but you never dream of becoming one. Instead of flying free, you go through the motions of a humdrum life with few joyful moments. When your days on earth finally come to an end, there is nothing to look forward to except going to your eternal rest in a quiet cocoon.

Now imagine being buried in the deadness of your circumstances without a flicker of hope. There is no struggle as you draw what you believe to be your very last breath. Then without warning, as death is reaching for you, God suddenly steps in and releases a new and powerful life force that causes you to break free from your shell of hopelessness. You clamber from your cocoon and step into a brand-new life. You have become what you never thought you would be: a new creation with wings to fly free.

Of course you recognize all of your old friends and loved ones, but to your horror, they don't seem to recognize you. Suddenly your wonderful transformation into a beautiful new creation is not as joyful as you hoped it would be. You begin to feel out of place in your new environment. Instead of being embraced by the people who once loved you, you find yourself facing criticism for being different and even being accused of thinking yourself superior just because you have wings and aren't crawling around on the ground anymore. A voice inside tells you that maybe you would have been better off if you had conformed instead of allowing yourself to be transformed.

It can be painful to hope for acceptance but to find rejection. That is why some people who are being transformed find themselves longing for their old life instead on rejoicing in the new. Little do you know that the Lord is using the walls of resistance that surround you to strengthen your wings and allow you to fly higher than you imagined.

The moral of the story is this: Transformation is not only the process of becoming a new creation, it is also a process of discovering a new place and purpose. It's the only way you can ever hope to rejoice in your transformation.

As in our story, the Lord will often use difficult circumstances that lead to isolation, rejection, and even the death of a particular lifestyle.

Once the woman in our story found her wings, she looked at her world through new eyes. Perhaps you had a similar experience when you accepted Jesus Christ and became a Christian. Suddenly your family members and friends treated you like you were an outsider. Going to church on Sunday and mid-week Bible study replaced your former social life. When you tried to talk to your old friends about the Scriptures or something that happened at church, they became annoyed, looking at you like you were speaking a foreign language.

Some of you might have experienced feelings of rejection and isolation on another level. Here's a good example of what I mean. Let's say you have been in church for many years. You have participated in all sorts of religious activities. You paid your tithes, attended worship services on a regular basis, and were well-liked and respected by your church members. But somewhere along the line, the Lord showed you that it wasn't enough for you to walk around playing the role of Susie Christian. In God's eyes, it was time for you to be used in a greater way, and it wasn't going to happen outside of a God-ordained transformation.

Whether the change took ten days or ten years, when the work was completed you were no longer an innocent babe sitting on the pew waiting for your spiritual leader to feed you the next bottle of the milk of the Word. Suddenly you began to see the preached Word of God as raw material that could be used to build God's kingdom here on earth.

Much to your surprise your new level of excitement left you feeling like an outsider in your own church. Not too many people understood the new you. They probably thought you were spooky because you didn't seem to have time for shopping and indulging in petty gossip anymore. The truth of the matter was that you found yourself preoccupied with the Lord, who was constantly whispering to you, when you were still, revealing to you the new plan and purpose that He had for your life.

Please understand that settling into your transformation is a journey in itself. There will be struggles and challenges coming from within your own heart, as well as from the people and things that surround you. It's almost like moving to a strange new city where no one wants to help you to find your way around. But eventually you meet people who, like yourself, have also been transformed. You discover this new city is a place where you can do things that only a transformed woman can do—you believe you can fly!

CHAPTER TEN

Setups That Lead to Setbacks

efore the woman in our story came to a place of contentment with God, she did not realize the dangers of her emotional and mental state. Her loneliness and frustration had left the door of her heart wide open to the temptations of Satan. I want to use the following Scripture to give you a sense of the range of emotions that the woman might have been feeling:

I am like a pelican of the wilderness;
  I am like an owl of the desert.
I lie awake,
  And am like a sparrow alone on the housetop. (Psalm 102:6–7)

Please note that the psalmist speaks here in reference to three different types of birds with three entirely different natures. The first bird is described as being in a wilderness, the second in a desert, and a third on a housetop. What wonderful imagery, especially when you investigate the nature of these three types of birds.[1] If you are wondering what this metaphor has to do with the human experience, then allow me to explain.

A pelican is a bird that feeds mostly on fish and therefore thrives near oceans and lakes. The wilderness is not the normal environment for a pelican. This bird is also accustomed to flying and swimming in a group formation. So strong is the pelican's commitment to its offspring that if there is no food available it will use its sharp beak to tear open its own flesh and allow its young to feed on the blood that flows from the open wound.

Like the pelican, you would sacrifice your own flesh for the people you love. Being alone in a wilderness, physical or emotional, is almost too much for you to handle. If you've ever had to be separated from the things that give your life meaning, then you know what it's like to have a wilderness experience. This bird feels isolated.

The owl faces another challenge. The desert is a place where it is difficult for owls to flourish. The reputation of the owl is one of wisdom, but wildlife specialists find that this is not so. The owl does not know how to build a strong nest. It also has a difficult time surviving pressures like food shortages.

Sometimes the people who are around you may think that you are wiser or stronger than you really are. They think you don't need a helping hand or moral support. To make matters worse, instead of swallowing your pride and asking for help, you are trying to live up to the reputation of being strong and wise. Deep inside you feel like the unwise owl. You don't know what to do or where to turn, so you sit all alone in a dry and barren desert. This bird feels inadequate.

The sparrow is a small bird that lacks color and brightness. It builds its nest close to the ground even though it can fly very high. This bird may seem common, colorless, even bland, but the Lord has given it a very special gift. The song sparrow and the lark sparrow have the ability to fill the heavens with songs—songs that it would seem could not possibly emanate from such small, dull-looking birds.

You may feel like you are not very special. Perhaps this lack of confidence makes you stay close to the ground even though you are capable of flying high. The people around you don't know about the significant talent that is hiding inside of you and you don't have the courage to expose your gift to the world. So instead of being on the inside where you are loved and accepted, you sit like a sparrow alone on a rooftop. This bird feels insignificant.

When the woman in our story watched the rain pour into her house, she probably experienced a spectrum of emotions that included isolation, inadequacy, and insignificance.

There are times when even the strongest Christians have moments of weakness and find themselves being set up for a setback. The enemy will wait until you are at your weakest point, then will send someone to help you—someone that, in spite of their "good intentions," will do more harm than good. The question I want to address is this: Can you recognize when you are being set up by the enemy? I believe that even in times of weakness you can learn to discern and to stand against the attack.

Don't be ignorant of Satan's devices. He hates those whom God has transformed. His greatest aim is to make you fall so he can discredit the work of God in your life. Like the woman in our story, sometimes it is after your greatest victories that Satan will launch the most devastating attack. Hopefully the following points will help you avoid being set up by the enemy.

GUARD YOUR MIND AND EMOTIONS

"Pssst! Want to try your luck?" It was the voice of a small-time hustler, who was standing outside Grand Central Station in New York City, playing a con game called three-card monte. I kept walking, because even a blind man could recognize that it was nothing more than a setup designed to rob people of time and money. Yet I was amazed to see that people were stopping and risking a few dollars in the hope of outsmarting this shady-looking man.

I hope you understand that Satan is no small time hustler. He's a smooth operator. He would never waste his time trying to lure you with a game of three-card monte. He would rather play for much higher stakes—your soul. One of the con games that Satan enjoys most is called playing-with-her-mind-and-emotions. For a woman, guarding her mind and mastering her emotions is the strongest defense against the attacks of the enemy. When he tries to lure her into one of his losing games, she must learn to smile and keep walking.

I often come in contact with Christians who really love the Lord, yet who indulge in what they view as harmless pastimes. R-rated movies filled with violence, profanity, and sexual messages often become a part of weekend relaxation for many Christians. Add to this corrupt music, books, magazines, videos, television, and Internet sites, and you have what I call a setup. When you expose your mind, emotions, and spirit to ungodly messages, don't be surprised when you find yourself considering fornication, adultery, or even violent actions against someone that has mistreated you.

Once you allow Satan access to your mind, he will invade your thoughts with ideas that emanate from the pit of hell. You may find yourself having perverted dreams or developing questions about your sexual preferences. Believe me, you are not some sort of freak just because you are thinking perverted thoughts. More likely you are simply a good person who has allowed Satan to enter through a door marked movies, Internet, television, paperback romances, and other forms of entertainment.

Let me remind you that exposure to the most subtle forms of eroticism or even "fun-loving" profanity is offensive to the Holy Spirit that dwells within you. The Scriptures give this warning: "Do not grieve the Holy Spirit of God, by whom you were sealed for the day of redemption" (Ephesians 4:30). Sin not only grieves the Holy Spirit, it separates you from friends and family members who choose to indulge in worldly entertainment.

Many times it isn't until after you get into trouble that you begin to connect the dots. By this I mean that you finally see the connection between the ungodliness that you allowed to settle in your mind and the actions that followed your pattern of thinking. That is why in Romans 12:2 you are called on to renew your mind. It has been my experience that the people who are most likely to reject certain types of entertainment and environments are usually those that either recognize their weaknesses or have experienced the consequences of exposing themselves to evil. King David made this declaration:

> I will set nothing wicked before my eyes;
> I hate the work of those who fall away;
> It shall not cling to me. (Psalm 101:3)

Don't Try to Play God with Sinners

I don't have enough fingers to count the women that have dated unsaved men in the hope that they would accept Christ and become faithful Christians and faithful mates. With hands lifted to the heavens these women pray to get married and live happily ever after. All too often the outcome is no laughing matter.

All of us can identify at least one woman whose husband went to church right up to the wedding. Once the couple married, however, the marriage turned into a living hell. Many women do not even make it to the altar. Instead of helping the man of her dreams find the Lord, she ends up raising a child alone.

Even sharing Christ with a friend or coworker takes a great deal of wisdom and discernment—especially when the negotiations begin. "I'll go to church with you if you come to a party with me." Eventually there will come a time when you will have to choose between your unsaved friends and your walk with the Lord. Be sure to recognize the voice of Satan when he tries to tell you, "If you want to win your friends to Christ, you must continue to hang out with them—even if they are drinking, using drugs, or doing other things that are offensive to God." Watch out—it's a setup!

Don't play God. You may not be as strong as you think you are. There is a real possibility that you will only find yourself getting caught up in the very things you were trying to escape. The best way to share your love for Jesus is to live a godly life. Stay away from the things that grieve the Holy Spirit.

I have a friend that was delivered from drugs and immediately separated himself from his old friends. Every weekend one of his old friends—who was still using drugs—would call him up and invite him to a party. To each invitation he responded with a flat refusal. After a while the calls stopped.

Then two years later, the calls started again with offers of wild parties and free drugs. My friend admitted that part of him still longed for his old life, but he stood his ground and turned down the invitations. Finally there came one last call. This time there was no party, just a request from the man who was always offering parties and drugs. "I'm calling you because I'm in the hospital with cancer," he said. "When I called those other times, there were no drugs or parties. You see, when you told me you had become a Christian, I had to make sure you were for real." On that same day my friend went to the hospital and led the dying man to the Lord.

The Word of God gives us this precious reminder: "Let your light so shine before men, that they may see your good works and glorify your Father in heaven" (Matthew 5:16).

LONERS ARE SATAN'S PRIME TARGETS

The greatest danger for the woman in our story was the growing isolation that filled her life. There was no one to whom she could relate or in whom to confide. The elders rejected her vision for the village and the women around her were only concerned with the things that affected their small circle of family and close friends.

It is unfortunate that the woman had not yet learned to fill the void by practicing the presence of God in her daily life—then she could have been comfortable around both babbling women and stuffy old men because she would not have been dependent upon either for her joy and contentment. She would have been able to accept them for what they were and not for what she needed them to be.

The Bible clearly spells out the importance of the covering and protection that comes from godly relationships:

> Think of ways to encourage one another to outbursts of love and good deeds. And let us not neglect our meeting together, as some people do, but encourage and warn each other, especially now that the day of his coming back again is drawing near. (Hebrews 10:24–25, NLT)

It is clear to me that God desires that we love, support, and encourage one another as a means of building our faith and protecting one another from satanic attacks. I am certain that is why Jesus sent His disciples out in twos (Luke 10:1). As they went out to battle the forces of evil, they needed a partner to cover them in prayer and watch for the traps of the enemy. I have often heard arguments from loners that they don't feel they have to go to church to have fellowship with God, or that they can't find any friends at the church they attend. They are being set up.

If God is doing a special work in your life and you feel that people cannot relate, pray for patience. If God is using you in a very special way, you need human support and fellowship, even if it is only one person who can discern your heart and pray with you and for you. Beware of becoming a loner. Remember: When wolves attack a flock of sheep, they start with the sheep that strays the farthest from the flock. Isolation may provide the perfect opportunity for Satan to come in and distort the plan of God. All because no one is around to help you stay on the right path.

While it is true that not going to church will not keep you out of heaven, it does hold a very important place in your social and spiritual development. If you are a Christian and you say you love God, then some sort of fellowship with like-minded believers should be a part of your life. After all, there certainly won't be any loners when you get to heaven. So if you are presently a Lone Ranger Christian who refuses to go to church, it's like saying, "My parents live close by, and I haven't been in their house in twenty years—but that doesn't mean I don't love them." Maybe you do love them, but something is wrong if you never set foot in their home.

Satan Has a Special Setup for Loners

I realize that many women have been wounded by church members and by pastors. In their pain, many of these women have concluded that all religious organizations are corrupt. If this has been your experience, let me take this time to encourage you to forgive the people who wounded you. The process of forgiveness is not only for their sake—it's for yours, too! Don't let Satan set you up by keeping you from a church family and building a monument of bitterness in your heart.

If you are not a loner but you recognize these characteristics in a woman you know, why not make yourself a committee of one dedicated to helping her come out of her shell? If this precious sister is allowed to withdraw completely, I assure you that the devil will plan a big setup for her.

There is another reason why certain people refuse to go to church or to fellowship with Christians: They don't like rules. They want to love God on their own terms and in their own way. They are offended when a preacher or teacher tells them that certain behavior is wrong, so they refuse to go to church because they don't want anyone, including God, to tell them how they should live. Rebellion is definitely a setup.

Loners tend to develop their own view of God and their own interpretation of the Word of God. They may even weave in bits of spiritual teachings from other religions that are in opposition to the Bible. They can't see it, but they are being set up. Many will end up in a cult or get involved in ungodly behavior and search for Scriptures to support their distorted view of things.

If you are in a church that has a good representation of your peer group and you still can't find one friend in a gathering of one hundred people, then you probably need a little help with your people skills. Here are some steps you can take.

First, find a smaller ministry or Bible study group where you can participate without feeling like you are under a lot of pressure.

Second, begin to pray about your personality type. If shyness is your challenge, recognize that timidity can either be a natural personality trait or it can be a mask for fear or pride. If you are too shy to speak in a public setting, ask questions, or pray, then you should try to uncover the source of your shyness. Ask the Lord to help you determine if you are actually afraid of rejection.

Maybe you demand such a high degree of perfection from yourself that your ego cannot endure the smallest chance of public failure. It may not be intentional, but pride can often masquerade itself as shyness.

I can recall going through a period where I failed to complete several important creative projects. I would get close to the end, then I would stop working. A close friend finally had a revelation about my peculiar behavior. "I think you're afraid of what people will say about your work. You are so full of pride that you would rather leave the project unfinished than take a chance that it might be viewed as less than perfect."

After thinking about what my friend had said, I was forced to admit that he was right. I wanted nothing less than perfection because then I would not only find acceptance, but I could also feel secretly superior to all the imperfect people in the world.

If you are a woman hiding her pride behind a mask of shyness, the devil can make your participation in one small event seem like a major undertaking. But what if the Holy Spirit moved you to pray or to share a Scripture with a person who was struggling, and you were too shy to do it? Would you let your shyness stand in the way of God's will? The Bible says, "The righteous are bold as a lion" (Proverbs 28:1b).

If you just don't like the idea of being out in front, please don't withdraw altogether. Think about working in the church nursery or with the children's ministry—there you usually don't have to worry about adult scrutiny. Find that one person you can trust and ask her to pray with you that you will be delivered from any hindrances your shyness creates. Whatever you do, don't withdraw: It's a setup.

LESSONS LEARNED FROM SETBACKS

At this point, you may be asking, "If God sees that I am lonely, feeling rejected, or facing tremendous pressure, why doesn't He come to my rescue? Why does He allow the enemy to take advantage of me during a time of weakness? Why does He allow me to go through setbacks?"

The bottom line is that there are certain things the Lord will allow you to experience in order to help you become a mature Christian. Here are some additional reasons why God allows us to experience setbacks.

God Uses Setbacks to Reveal Your Weaknesses

When you come to Christ, all the baggage from the past comes with you. You tend to want to hold on to your possessions even if you are moving to a better place. But how would it look if you were moving into a beautiful, spacious, new house but you wanted to keep the broken-down furniture from your old apartment? The furniture may not fit into your lovely new home, but if you are attached to it or if it's just too comfortable, you'll desire to keep it around.

In the same way, when you are going through the process of transformation, you still have a tendency to hold on to baggage from your past. It can be the baggage of past relationships, worldly friends and activities, unforgiveness, or immoral behavior. No matter how hard you try, you can't make your old baggage fit into your new life in Christ.

When God removes the baggage that keeps you from maturing, you may cry like a baby whose bottle has been taken away. Despite your anger and frustration, God knows that it's time for you to grow up. He would rather allow you to fall and learn from your failure than to protect you from your weaknesses, knowing you might be destroyed by them further down the road.

You may be a woman who has been a committed Christian for many years yet are still carrying baggage from the past. You may have lived with the remnants of character flaws and weaknesses for such a long time that you may believe God is going to leave you the way you are. You may not realize it, but when you say you are a Christian and people encounter your baggage—maybe you're selfish, greedy, or unhappy—they may conclude that all Christians are that way. The longer you are a Christian, the more the Lord wants you to have a testimony of being a joyful, compassionate, woman of integrity.

Maybe you have cried out for the Lord to change you into the person He desires you to become. That's like asking a contractor to remodel your house. You sign the agreement, pay the money, and watch the process begin. At first you might be horrified when the contractor starts tearing out walls and ripping up floors, but he assures you that he can't do the new alterations without destroying the old design.

I have been a Christian for many years, and God's not finished with me yet. Just when I think the Lord has forgotten all about the old baggage I've been dragging around, one day He'll back up a dump truck and haul away the "junk." He begins His work by reminding me that as long as I am bound by the smallest ungodly trait, I am bringing dishonor to the name of Jesus. I am also doing a disservice to myself and to the people around me.

The longer we walk with Christ, the more our weaknesses will begin to surface—and believe me, we all have them. Even the weaknesses that you thought were completely gone will make an attempt to resurface from time to time. You may become angry or demonstrate behavior that you haven't displayed in years. The weaknesses can include bitterness, deception, idolatry, fornication, and adultery—you know what they are in your life. Any of these can make for a painful fall and bring embarrassment and harsh consequences.

On the other hand, sometimes a fall is the fastest road to deliverance. Even if you have to lose things that are precious or have to start at square one in rebuilding your life, the Lord would rather have you go through that painful process of revealing your sin than allow you the grow into a big spiritual fake.

The woman in our story became of woman of power, graciousness, and integrity as the Lord continued His work. Whatever you are going through may feel like a setback, but it's really a remodeling job that will eventually make you more like Jesus. "For whom He foreknew, He also predestined to be conformed to the image of His Son" (Romans 8:29a).

Your Love for God Will Grow Stronger

After falling prey to desire, the woman in our story grieved because she had sinned against God. To make matters worse, the devil was always nearby to remind her of her failure.

Many people grow up hearing about the wrath of God's judgment against sinners, but most don't hear that the Bible also tells us, "The LORD is merciful and gracious, Slow to anger, and abounding in mercy" (Psalm 103:8). He proves this by allowing us to have setbacks. Our failures actually serve to make us stronger and more grateful to the Lord for His goodness.

There is a wonderful Bible story that demonstrates the mercy of God. A fallen woman in search of a new life encountered Jesus while He was dining with a group of Pharisees. Though the Pharisees were angered by the presence of this sinful woman, she ignored them. She fell on her knees and wept with repentance, kissing the feet of Jesus. In her hands she carried an alabaster flask filled with expensive perfumed oil. After washing His feet with her tears and drying them with her hair, she anointed the feet of Jesus with the precious oil.

Jesus knew the Pharisees were wondering why He allowed this sinful woman to touch Him. After a gentle rebuke for their piety, Jesus told them that this woman's love and gratitude were great because her sins had been so great. Jesus did not ask the woman about her past. "He said to her, 'Your sins are forgiven'" (Luke 7:48).

Sometimes those who love the Lord most are those who have fallen the hardest. The Lord called King David "a man after His own heart," yet David committed adultery with Bathsheba and murdered her husband. How's that for a great big fall? But Psalm 51 presents strong evidence that David did not continue in sin. His love for God was so great that He could not bear to lose fellowship with the Lord. Listen to David repent with his whole heart:

Have mercy upon me, O God,
        According to Your lovingkindness;
    According to the multitude of Your tender mercies,
        Blot out my transgressions.

Wash me thoroughly from my iniquity,
And cleanse me from my sin. (Psalm 51:1–2)

If you sin greatly then return to God in complete repentance, the Lord does not want to condemn you. His desire is to help you to your feet, even though He knows that you may fall again and again. As time passes and you continue to rise from your setbacks, your love will shine like a burning ember in the midst of a crowd of lukewarm Christians who probably have never committed any "big" sin, only "little" sins, leaving them with "little" love. These people fail to recognize that in the sight of God we are all sinners saved by His abundant grace.

The Scriptures tell us that the Lord takes no delight in lukewarm Christians: "So then, because you are lukewarm, and neither cold nor hot, I will vomit you out of My mouth" (Revelation 3:16). That is why some of the greatest redeemed sinners become champions for God—their love for Him is red hot. The Lord is looking for women who are broken over their sin and so grateful for their deliverance that they are overflowing with love for Him.

God Wants You to Have Compassion for Others

Sometimes when a woman becomes a mature Christian she forgets about the vulnerabilities and weaknesses that can lure her into sin. She perceives herself as invincible, and if she is not careful she will find herself less than sympathetic to the failures of others. This is another important reason why we must never delude ourselves into thinking that we have "arrived" when it comes to being perfect Christians.

The devil can easily set you up if you allow yourself to forget what it's like to go through a spiritual battle. But just like the woman in our story, God may first allow you to experience a "leaky roof," then suddenly to discover your world caving in on you.

The Lord will use the tool of painful experience to continue His transforming work. Your listening will become longer and your speech shorter. You will pray as if the person is drowning and only God can save her. The Scriptures you offer will not be dead words that have no power; rather, they will bring hope because they are offered from a heart filled with love. When He is finished you will have developed a whole new level of compassion for those that are struggling with sin. When you encounter people enduring emotional or spiritual battles, your attitude will be different.

To keep yourself from the setup of spiritual amnesia, I encourage you to rehearse your testimony on a regular basis. Never allow yourself to forget what life would be like without Christ. Recount aloud the miracles that He has performed to bring you to where you are now. Remind yourself that you are a sinner saved by grace.

Perhaps you grew up in a Christian home and it is difficult for you to appreciate what it is like to live without the love of Jesus. You may even resent your quiet, "goody-goody" life, or—at the opposite end of the spectrum—you may look down on those who do not demonstrate godly behavior. Before the Lord topples your pedestal, I encourage you to step down and spend time with people that are living without the Lord.

The devil may deceive you into thinking that you missed all the fun because you didn't have a string of lovers or weren't free to "do your own thing." If that's a nagging thought in your mind, maybe you should spend part of the summer performing missionary work. When you encounter broken families and all the other things that come with a godless life you will understand the emptiness and despair felt by people that live without Jesus. Perhaps such an encounter will help you to realize how blessed you are to know the Lord.

One of the great failures of the church is its tendency to look down on people that have come out of sinful pasts. I pray that you will not have to experience a setback to realize that as a Christian you are nothing more than a recipient of the grace of God.

> For I say, through the grace given to me, to everyone who is among you, not to think of himself more highly than he ought to think, but to think soberly, as God has dealt to each one a measure of faith. (Romans 12:3)

I strongly recommend that you take the time to examine yourself and make certain that you are standing in a place of mercy and compassion toward others: "Therefore let [her] who thinks [she] stands take heed lest [she] fall" (1 Corinthians 10:12).

God Knows That Experience Is Your Best Teacher

When it comes to the learning process, some people do very well reading books and following directions. Others, like myself, learn quicker with hands-on experience. No one knows your temperament better than the One who created you. God knows that some of His little girls are strong-willed children. If this strength is channeled in the right direction, the strong-willed woman can do great things for the kingdom of God.

The Lord needs women who are not easily intimidated by the devil. When you are strong-willed, the enemy will try extra hard to block you—especially as you become more determined to move forward. But if you do not allow the Lord to harness your power, determination, and fearlessness, your gift can become destructive rather than constructive.

That is why from God's perspective you sound like a whining little kid that says things like, "But my sister did something wrong and You didn't spank her—You only gave her a time-out. Why do You treat me so mean and treat other people so nice?"

How well I know the answer to that childlike question. Yes, I am a strong-willed woman, too. I have personally experienced the lengths that God will go to to demonstrate His fatherly love (I am smiling as I write this). He knows what it takes to get my attention, to make me broken and pliable to His will.

Maybe you're more of a gentle lady. Perhaps all it takes is a whisper from the Lord to turn your heart from the wrong path. For the rest of us—and we know whom we are—the Lord will give a few strong warnings. He already knows you won't listen, but His justice demands He give you the same opportunity to repent that He extends to others. After you ignore all the warnings, the Lord steps back and allows you to stop by the closest Burger King of life and "have it your way."

When the consequences of your actions bring you to a place of repentance, you will hopefully come to understand that you can't break God's laws without God's laws breaking you. Once you are back on the right track, albeit broken and sometimes bruised, you can warn others to beware of the setups so they will never have to receive the miserable payment for the wages of sin. Like the woman in our story, after you have been tried in the furnace of affliction you are a perfect weapon, ready to be used by the Lord. God's objective is to turn weaknesses into Christ-centered strengths.

God Wants You to Continue to Be God-Dependent

Although the Bible usually depicts the women of Israel as passive and submissive, there were some women who were strong-willed and independent. Sarah, the wife of Abraham, was a woman who knew how to take control. When the Lord delayed in sending her a child, Sarah made arrangements for her Egyptian maid, Hagar, to bear a son for Abraham. Of course her plan backfired, because Hagar was as strong-willed as Sarah. There was so much strife between them after Hagar gave birth to a son (Ishmael) that Sarah insisted Abraham kick the woman and her child out of their house.

Little did Sarah know that her impatience and her strong will were the setup for a conflict that continues to rage between the Arabs (the descendants of Ishmael, son of Hagar) and the Jews (the descendants of Isaac, son of Sarah). Even after Sarah had suffered the consequences of refusing to be God-dependent, the Lord still did not go back on His plan to bless her.

Like Sarah, maybe you know what it's like to deceive yourself into thinking that the Lord is in control of your life, when in reality you are back in the driver's seat. You are no longer allowing God to lead you; instead, you are doing the leading and asking God to go with you.

The speech of a woman in denial might sound something like Sarah's plan to use Hagar to bear children for Abraham: "The Lord has opened a door for me to work on a project in Japan. I know I have a new baby and all, but my husband and I have found a wonderful live-in housekeeper. Now when I'm in Japan and my husband is commuting to Washington, this wonderful housekeeper—whom the Lord has sent into our lives—will be watching our new baby."

I'm not saying that the Lord can't work in this way, but before you convince yourself that your plans are from God, maybe you should bow at the altar of godly wisdom and pray about your plan. I want you to know that the speech I just presented is not something I made up. I did change a few minor details, but it's a true story. In an attempt to justify their actions, Christians are making their own decisions and then saying, the Lord told me.

I want to offer you three basic principles that will help you discern whether your actions reflect God-dependence or independence of God. First, the decision you make should line up with the Word of God. Second, however the Lord leads you, He will clearly confirm whether you are on the right or wrong track. And third, make sure you are submitted to a pastor or a seasoned Christian friend to help you make godly decisions.

Like many Christians, when you first entered into a relationship with the Lord, you probably went to church or joined a Bible study so you could learn how to know the will of God for your life and become an obedient servant. The Lord may have even allowed a circumstance in which you could do nothing but depend on Him. Even as you learned to trust that the Lord is faithful and trustworthy, your old do-it-yourself nature was always waiting in the wings. Once your life became a little more comfortable, you learned how to play the Christian game—the one where you speak and act as if you are dependent upon God when in truth it's you that's calling the shots.

Without a strong system of checks and balances, old behavioral patterns can creep into your life. If you are not prayerful, your old nature will rise up and say, "Why wait on the Lord when I can do this myself? If God didn't want me to make my own decisions, He would not have given me a mind to think with."

If you are not able to discern the voice of satanic manipulation within your own heart, then God might allow you to go experience difficulty to get you back on track. After facing the repercussions of your independent decision-making, you will gladly return to God-dependence. The greatest risk you face is the possibility of missing out on God's perfect will and setting something in motion that you will live to regret.

Continue to obey and pray; the Lord will lead you into His perfect will.

CHAPTER ELEVEN

The Rules of Contentment

The woman in our story found herself alone in the world, searching for a place of contentment and rest. No matter how hard she tried, she could not find a place to hide from the many uncertainties she was facing. Though she was surrounded by people, no one could offer the emotional refuge she so desperately needed. As a quiet storm raged in her heart, she faced a brand-new enemy: discontentment. Once Satan grips our souls with discontentment, he drains us of our inner strength and leaves us frustrated and restless.

The search for contentment is like the feeling you get after being on a long trip: You can't wait to get home to your own house and your own bed. While enduring an uncomfortable flight or waiting for your ride to pick you up, you dream about relaxing in your bathtub and stretching out on crisp, clean sheets.

It may not take a long trip to stir up images of that one place where you can find peace and contentment. A hard day at school or work can leave you counting down the minutes and seconds until you can make a dash for the door.

Home was meant to be the place that represents refuge and contentment. It may not look like something out of *Better Homes and Gardens*, but the possessions that fill that place are an extension of yourself. It feels so good to be surrounded by familiar and comfortable things. Sometimes if you've been at home all day, family time and related activities can make you long for the sun to go down and for all the little and big people to settle into sleep. Then you can steal into the kitchen, bathroom, or den, close your eyes, and thank God for a few precious moments of contentment.

Just as home represents a place where you should be able to escape and find contentment in the natural realm, there should also be a place in the spiritual realm to which you can retreat and find rest and contentment from the struggles of this life. If you are wise you will not allow your soul to find its contentment in the things of this world. One tornado ripping through your house, marriage, romance, friendship, or job can leave your soul naked and your contentment in ruins.

There should be a spiritual dwelling place inside of you that cannot be disturbed by the cares of this life. Your spiritual home should be filled with the possessions that reflect your truest self. You should be able to kick off your shoes and allow your spirit to find contentment no matter what kind of crazy things are going on in the natural realm. These "possessions" should include pictures of the blessings of the Lord, all of them beautifully framed in your heart. The Word of God should reside with you like a soft, clean bed upon which you can stretch out and luxuriate in the promises of God. When the storms of life are cold and raging, you can stand by the fireplace of the Holy Spirit with a blanket of contentment covering your soul.

LONELINESS—THE ROAD TO DISCONTENTMENT

Have you ever stood in the midst of a sea of people yet felt like you were all alone in the world? At one time or another, most of us have had to deal with feelings of loneliness. These feelings can make you extremely vulnerable to the attacks of the enemy. Discontentment is an enemy that attacks from the inside rather than the outside. You may appear to be happy and secure, but if you have no peace and contentment on the inside, it is like being defenseless in a vast wilderness filled with predators.

I want to make one thing perfectly clear: Contrary to popular opinion, you don't have to be a single woman to feel alone and dissatisfied. All too often I meet married women that live in homes complete with husbands and children yet are consumed by discontentment and loneliness.

If you are a single woman operating under the delusion that marriage will take away your feelings of loneliness, it's time to stop dreaming. A married woman can face the same challenges. She might find herself physically separated from her husband because of work, school, military service, incarceration—any number of things. She might also find herself living under the same roof yet emotionally separated from him. Major issues—infidelity, poor communication, financial troubles, child-rearing challenges, and spiritual differences—can all serve to drive a wedge between couples.

Whether you are single or married, you may encounter isolation in any number of settings: in the workplace, at school, or while pursuing some social cause. This is especially true if you are facing gender, racial, or religious discrimination. Whatever the reason, you may be left to fend off feelings of discontentment and abandonment.

I can picture two women standing outside of a church, carrying on a friendly—yet competitive—dialogue. The married woman is holding her young son by the hand; they are waiting for her husband, who is taking care of some business in the pastor's office. The unmarried woman greets her with a Miss-America sort of wave. Instead of holding a child by the hand, she carries an expensive designer purse.

The married woman gazes longingly at the designer purse, which she can no longer afford, since she and her husband are experiencing some financial difficulties. The single woman is drooling over the cute little boy, wishing desperately that he belonged to her.

"So, where have you been hiding?" the married woman asks.

"I just returned from a trip to Europe," the single woman answers. "And what have you been up to?"

"Oh, my husband and I just celebrated another wedding anniversary. He took me out for a candlelit dinner," she says, smiling. "I am so glad I married him."

The two women say good-bye, giving each other a peck on the cheek. Then both of them walk away, each feeling frustrated. *Lord, why don't I have a husband and a beautiful child?* the unmarried woman thinks as she starts her BMW.

Lord, why can't I have beautiful clothes, drive a nice car, and see the world? the married woman wonders as she and her husband sit in their old car, trying to get the engine to turn over.

It is important to recognize the hand of God in every situation. Just as the Lord works to build your spiritual muscles, He also wants you to have emotional endurance. God wants you to stand against the attacks of the enemy, whether they be internal or external. He wants you to embrace contentment in every situation. The apostle Paul put it this way:

Not that I speak in regard to need, for I have learned in whatever state I am, to be content: I know how to be abased, and I know how to abound. Everywhere and in all things I have learned both to be full and to be hungry, both to abound and to suffer need. I can do all things through Christ who strengthens me. (Philippians 4:11–13)

Every time I read this passage it is a "praise the Lord" moment. In my way of thinking, the greatest gift we could ever receive from God is the gift of contentment. Paul reminds us that we must *learn* to be content—to find peace and satisfaction regardless of the circumstances. If the single woman and the married woman in our little story had learned the secret of contentment, they could have enjoyed a relationship built on mutual honesty and support. Instead, they chose to stew silently in a big pot of envy, rivalry, and discontentment.

It is my hope that this scenario will better help you understand why God wants us to learn the importance of finding contentment. He works best in the classroom of challenging circumstances. That is where He teaches us the rules of contentment. If you are single, He wants you to learn to enjoy all the advantages of being single; if you are married, He wants you to develop the skills to enjoy all the advantages of being married. You can *learn* to be content with your career, your financial situation, and any area of your life.

Please know that I am not saying you should accept a difficult marriage without trying to make it better. I am not saying that you should stop looking forward to being married. I am not saying that you shouldn't try to make advancements in your job, education, or any other areas of your life. What I am saying is that God wants you to learn to have contentment, no matter what transition you may be going through. If you don't learn contentment in all things then you will live a frustrated life or, like the woman in our opening story, the lure of sin will cause you to stumble and fall into a state of discontentment that is more painful than what you are already experiencing.

LESSONS IN CONTENTMENT

Let me remind you that the Lord uses challenges to help you learn the rules of contentment. The following rules are designed to help you learn to be content.

Learn How to Have Conversations with God

Most Christians make prayer a part of their daily lives, to some degree or another. However, too few Christians know how to have a *conversation* with God. The Bible is filled with stories of men and women who had such conversations. Perhaps you have experienced this yourself, but those wondrous dialogues have been too few and far between. You might have treated those times like they were miraculous events instead of as conversations that could become a part of your life that is familiar and comfortable.

In the natural realm, when you are feeling lonely or rejected you immediately look for someone to talk to or for a shoulder to cry on. In those lonely times when you pick up the phone and call a friend, know that the Lord would love for you to have the same type of relationship with Him. He wants to talk with you one on one so that you can experience the power of His presence. The Scriptures tell us that "in [God's] presence is fullness of joy" (Psalm 16:11). God's joy is so fulfilling that when He comes near there is no room left for loneliness or discontentment. Unfortunately, it is all too easy to block out the comfort of His presence with the distraction of a noisy television or by carrying on a telephone conversation with someone who is probably more lonely and frustrated than you.

A dear friend who is a single mom told me the story of how she was lying in her bed one night feeling very lonely. She began whispering to the Lord, telling Him her feelings. The Lord's presence filled the room and then He spoke to her heart: *You don't have to be lonely. I am here with you.* My friend said that her sadness gradually disappeared. She went to sleep with a joyful heart and a smile on her face.

Remember that lasting contentment can only be found in the presence of God. As you seek it, spiritual warfare will continue to rage over the territory of your emotions, and whoever has the greatest presence will win the battle. When you feed your loneliness with sad movies, reckless spending, drugs, binge eating, wrong relationships, or whatever else the enemy can talk you into, for a short period of time you will find relief. But when it's time to pay for your folly, you will find yourself in a worse state than at the beginning.

It is just the opposite when you spend time with the Lord. Conversations with God not only fill you with peace, joy, and contentment, but when you take the time to listen to His still, small voice, He will show you how to fill the void in a way that is practical and productive. Conversations with the Lord leave no room for the invasion of loneliness.

Before my mother went to be with the Lord, I used to walk by her bedroom and hear her whispering. I would stick my head through the doorway and ask if she wanted company. I remember her smiling, yet at the same time looking like I was interrupting something important. "I already have company," she replied. "I was having a visit with the Lord."

Learn How to Give Yourself Away

The national anthem of lonely people goes something like this: "I'm so *bored*. My husband acts like I'm not alive. My children are doing their own thing. I have no one to love and I can't find anything to do except sit here feeling lonely."

If you are one of those wonderful people who claims that Jesus is the center of your life, then why are you so unhappy? Your thoughts might be getting a bit tangled as you try to tell yourself that you do love Jesus but you can't seem to find joy and contentment. I can almost see God shaking His head, saying, "I have a great idea. If you're lonely, why not find someone who would love to share some of your time?"

I can see you sitting there with a look of wonder in your eyes. "Where can I find someone who wants my company and my love?" The answer is easy. There are people everywhere in need of the love that you have to give. You can give your love by teaching a Sunday school class, for instance. I guarantee that if you really get involved with kids you will never be bored, lonely, or without love. There are elderly people shut away in homes who would love for you to bring them flowers, sing them a song, or take them for a walk. There is no excuse for a person who has experienced the love of God to be unwilling to open her heart and share her love with others.

When you give yourself away to someone less blessed than yourself, the Lord will give you a new appreciation for the blessings you have been ignoring. When you visit prisons, you will find yourself thanking God for your freedom and for leading you in the right path. If you work with mentally or physically challenged people, you will find yourself thanking God for a healthy mind and body. Contentment will slowly flood your spirit and soul.

But if you choose to participate in selective love, then maybe it is not love that you are really seeking. If you want someone just to love you back, then you may not fully understand how love works. The true spirit of love does not look to receive from others. Real love finds contentment in giving love to anyone who needs it. The greatest desire of real love is to continuously give itself away. "For God so loved the world that He gave His only begotten Son, that whoever believes in Him should not perish but have everlasting life" (John 3:16).

Learn That You Are Responsible for Your Contentment

How many times have you heard someone say, "I'll die if you leave me—I can't live without you." While I certainly understand the power of emotional attachments, life and death should never be part of your emotional equation. If Satan knows that you "worship" the love of another person, sooner or later he will take advantage of your emotional state.

To make matters worse, if God sees that your love for a person has moved to a level of adoration greater than your love for Him, He might just allow Satan to have a field day with your emotions. The Lord would allow this to teach you that real contentment can only be found in Him: "But where are your gods that you have made for yourselves? Let them arise, If they can save you in the time of your trouble" (Jeremiah 2:28a).

It is just as important that you do not become so emotionally dependent that you make a prisoner of your husband, boyfriend, child, coworker, spiritual leader, or friend. All too often lawsuits arise in the workplace because someone crosses the line in search of emotional comfort that is not in the job description. A secretary finds herself playing baby-sitter, wife, or mother to her boss; an employer must begin counseling a worker that is demonstrating destructive or nonproductive behavior; a teacher crosses the line with a student—each of these behaviors is an attempt to fill the void of discontentment.

A person dwelling in a place of discontentment can experience the kind of mental breakdown that causes him to walk into a high school and kill his classmates or to commit some terrible act against the very people he claims to love.

You must be very careful that your contentment is not based on expectations that will end in failure. Unrealistic expectations lead to unmet goals. Unmet goals lead to frustration and disappointment. Frustration and disappointment lead to bitterness, then anger, then rage. Perhaps it would be a good idea to share your expectations with someone who can give you wise counsel; if your expectations are rooted in fantasy and not fact, you can regroup and save yourself needless heartache. When your contentment comes from the Lord, you can accept disappointments without falling apart.

What if the person who is sharing your life has a bad day (or week, or month) and doesn't feel like catering to your emotional needs? Are you going to sink into a pit of depression or think of ending your life? I know women who build emotional prisons in which they incarcerate the people they claim to love. When those people struggle to escape their grasp, they sound the alarm and begin the hunt to recapture them.

For some, it may be a difficult lesson to learn how to freely love a person without making him or her responsible for your happiness; once again, when you are filled with the love of God, you can love the people God sends into your life without draining or consuming them. It is important to realize that no one is responsible for your contentment but yourself.

I make it a priority to identify the simple decisions that safeguard my contentment. I have come to a place in my life where I watch out for the things that can steal my contentment, because I now realize that contentment is a rare and valuable gift. People and opportunities will try to get you to sacrifice your contentment or to exchange it for wealth or power. Even imitation love will try to steal your contentment and leave you bankrupt.

I've installed a full security system—complete with sensors—just in case a thief is lurking about. If something crosses that invisible line attempting to steal my contentment, the alarm goes off immediately. Contentment is such a valuable gift that I practice the following rules to ensure that I will never lose my wonderful blessings:

- Spend time with God every morning
- Spend time with family: listen; encourage; don't criticize
- Be slow to anger and quick to forgive
- Don't measure wealth by possessions
- Make what you love doing a part of your life's work
- Take a daily walk/exercise/nap
- Plan your schedule so you don't have to rush
- Avoid negative communication
- Don't be afraid of change, or of trying new things
- Have one friend who can make you laugh

Learn How to Focus on the Positives

I remember a time just before Christmas one year when my two daughters and I decided to have a Christmas brunch. We prepared a menu then went our separate ways with an understanding of who would be bringing which dishes and what time the family would be arriving. On Christmas Eve I stayed up late preparing food for the following morning. I fixed a large salmon stuffed with seafood dressing, I baked bread and pies, and I made eggnog and several other family favorites. The brunch was scheduled for 11 A.M.

It was 1 P.M. when the first family members arrived, explaining that they hadn't had time to prepare the dishes they had promised to bring. At that point I could have been the national poster girl for discontentment. Without a doubt it was the worst Christmas ever, complete with burnt waffles and runny omelets. Instead of focusing on the fact that my family was all together and in good health, I refused to let go of my expectations for the day. I focused instead on the negative—what I perceived as my ruined Christmas brunch.

For the most part, the family ignored my state of discontentment. They ate cold (or microwaved) food and drank warm (instead of chilled) eggnog, all the time laughing, talking, taking pictures, and exchanging gifts.

By the following Christmas I had repented of my negative attitude. Just before the holiday, my oldest daughter suggested, with a big smile on her face, "We had so much fun last Christmas, why don't we have another brunch?"

All eyes swiveled in my direction for a final verdict. "Sounds great!" I exclaimed. On Christmas Eve, I fixed a few dishes, set the table, and went to bed. Of course the next morning my youngest daughter called to let me know she was running late. I wasn't the least bit upset because I had a brand-new plan and a brand-new attitude. I prepared the food and set it out on the table; it was ready for anyone who might show up wanting to sample my Christmas goodies. I did not lock myself into a place in which my contentment depended on other people to meet my expectations. God is the only one who will never fail.

When you focus on the negative experiences of the past, you can miss out on the blessings of the present. When God tries to channel you toward new blessings, you may find yourself unable to receive them because you are negatively focused. If you are not careful, Satan will fill your thoughts with a long list of disappointments and offenses that everyone else has forgotten except you. I learned a long time ago that when you rehearse past offenses over and over again, it produces a substance in your spirit called bitterness.

The only way to find peace and contentment is to give Satan his eviction notice. Let him know that he can no longer sit around and play his loud music featuring the "somebody's done me wrong" song. Nor should the devil be allowed to live rent free in your emotions, stirring up negative thoughts whenever he feels like it.

The next time the enemy tries to pop in a video featuring the memory of a negative event, stop the thought immediately. Eject the tape. Switch the tape to images of all the times the Lord has blessed you when you didn't deserved to be blessed. Things may not be the way you desire them at the present moment, but you can find contentment by turning your thoughts to the small blessings and to His promise of bigger blessings still to come.

Thank God for His goodness and for not allowing the difficulties in your life to be worse than they are. Then focus on the faithfulness of His Word, for He has promised to work things out in your life. Know that just as He is in your thoughts, you are also in His thoughts:

Many, O LORD my God, are Your wonderful works
    Which You have done;
And Your thoughts toward us

Cannot be recounted to You in order;
    If I would declare and speak of them,
        They are more than can be numbered. (Psalm 40:5)

Learn to Recognize and Refuse False Contentment

We cannot turn on the television or pick up a magazine without being bombarded by advertisements promising contentment: fad diets that will take away the frustration of being overweight; dating services that provide opportunities to meet your dream mate; financial empowerment conferences that will bring your money worries to an end. Business—legal and illegal, moral and immoral—thrives on the human need for contentment.

The book of Hebrews warns the early Christians to beware the snares of false contentment. "Let your conduct be without covetousness; be content with such things as you have. For He Himself has said, 'I will never leave you nor forsake you'" (Hebrews 13:5). Let me offer a loose translation of what the writer of this passage is really saying: "Don't be greedy for things; be content with what you have. God is all you need. He will never fail to satisfy you."

You might ask, "But how does God go about meeting my emotional needs?" I can tell you from my own experience that the closer you draw to Him, the closer He draws near to you. Go to a church where you are fed the Word of God. Get involved in Bible studies. Join a ministry where God can use you. As you grow closer and closer to Him, you will feel contentment filling every void in your life: "Draw near to God and He will draw near to you" (James 4:8a).

The challenge you face in your search for contentment can be sabotaged by greed. Though most of us struggle with greed on some level, the greed I'm talking about right now may not come from your own heart but from the high-tech advertisers who are experts at stirring up your appetite for things that you once had no interest in attaining. Something is always coming along that is bigger, better, or newer, making what you already have seem obsolete. This applies even to people you love.

It is important that in your times of prayer you ask the Lord to protect your heart from the spirit of greed that is prevailing in our society and to help you find satisfaction in the simple pleasures of life.

Your pursuit of false contentment may not always be triggered by greed. It could arise from a deep need or hurt. If you are experiencing emotional pain, you need relief. If you don't know how to tap into the contentment that comes from God, you will look for something to anesthetize your suffering. If you have ever been high on pills or alcohol, then you know how numb you feel in a drug-induced stupor. The problem with satanically inspired contentment, though, is that it never lasts. It leaves you with the need for "more" and always in greater doses than were previously necessary. This is how people find themselves on the pathway to addiction.

There are other forms of false contentment. You can become content with living in poverty because the enemy has persuaded you that you are not capable of achieving anything better. *Lack* is a spiritual enemy. It is not God's will for you to be content with hunger and unemployment. The Lord does not want you to be content by accepting the idea that your needs are simply not going to be met. Rather, He wants you to be content by having the faith that He will supply all of your needs by showing you the way to rise out of poverty. The apostle Paul said it this way: "My God shall supply all your need according to His riches in glory by Christ Jesus" (Philippians 4:19). God can meet all your needs, whether they be emotional, physical, spiritual, or material.

In our contemporary world there are many false options promising contentment. If you have never experienced the full outpouring of contentment that comes from the Lord, you might persuade yourself that you're better off chasing the elusive blue bird of happiness. In the popular movie *Jerry McGuire,* the lead character makes a statement that still lingers in the hearts of many as one of the great romantic quotes of our age. Jerry looks deeply into the eyes of his love interest and says simply, "You complete me."

If you are looking for a person to complete you, it will be like setting up housekeeping in an igloo in the middle of July: It just won't last. Allow me to share a few words from the book of Colossians on the subject of completeness:

> Beware lest anyone cheat you through philosophy and empty deceit, according to the tradition of men, according to the basic principles of the world, and not according to Christ. For in Him dwells all the fullness of the Godhead bodily; and you are complete in Him, who is the head of all principality and power. (Colossians 2:8–10)

As contentment becomes a way of life, you will be equipped to accomplish great things for God—things that only a woman can do.

CHAPTER TWELVE

Following God's Vision for Your Life

The woman in our opening story went through a season when she felt as though she were moving blindly with no understanding of what God was doing in her life. Then one morning while praying she had a vision so clear that she knew without a doubt the Lord was speaking to her heart.

Sometimes the Lord reveals things that you don't want to know, but it is important to remember that He sees the big picture. I am sure the woman would have been a lot happier if God had given her a vision of financial success or of the new husband He would be bringing into her life. But instead of the vision she longed for, the Lord showed her the evil herdsmen and the poisoned meat.

The woman did what most of us do when God reveals something we don't want to know: She argued and complained. She behaved like Moses, who didn't want to go to Pharaoh, or like the prophet Habakkuk, who asked, "Why do You show me iniquity, and cause me to see trouble?" (Habakkuk 1:3a).

Even though He revealed a difficult challenge, her decision to obey Him was directly connected to her desire for a wonderful plan that she could not see. As she continued to follow God's vision for her life, it eventually led her to a place where her gifts and talents were appreciated and used to the fullest. God's plan also led her to the man who would become her husband.

There are two ways to define vision. The first type of vision comes from the knowledge we receive from the preached Word—"Where there is no vision, the people perish" (Proverbs 29:18a, KJV). As we submit ourselves to the teaching of God's Word, we receive direction (i.e., vision) for our lives. The second definition of vision is the idea that God reveals His will through direct communication to our hearts and minds.

God speaks to people in many ways. To certain people His guidance comes through piercing insights into specific Scriptures; others He guides through strong impressions that go beyond mere thoughts; still others seem able to hear His still, small voice better than the rest of us can; and for some, He grants visions in the form of dreams or mental imagery.

There are times when God works this way with me. He gives me a special ability to see visions of His will. I don't pretend to understand why He does this—nor do I mean to say that if you're not having these remarkable visions from God then you're doing something wrong. Just as Jesus never healed in the same way twice, so He doesn't lead us all in the same manner. Our heavenly Father delights in variety.

One of the most unforgettable events of my life took place shortly after I had become a Christian. I was attending my first prayer conference at the Lake Arrowhead Retreat Center in southern California. I had never spent so much time in prayer! I can still remember being filled with so many unexplainable emotions that all I could do was walk around the beautiful grounds praising the Lord.

On the last evening of the conference we held an all-night prayer meeting. A multitude of voices filled the sanctuary with Scripture readings, songs, tears, confession, and prayers of thanksgiving. The atmosphere was so charged with the presence of God that I had to kneel down by my chair, close my eyes, and weep.

A short time after I had bowed in prayer, a picture began to form in my mind. It was as if I were looking up at the sky and the heavens were filled with billowing clouds that were slowly moving toward me. As the clouds grew closer, the images began to change into a sea of angels dressed in glowing white robes. The angels were coming from every direction—thousands and thousands of them singing and praising God.

Suddenly the host of angels parted, and there came a light so bright that I was forced to look away for a moment. When I looked back, I saw the image of Jesus sitting on a throne. I felt as though I were suspended in time. I bowed before the King of kings and Lord of lords. I could have stayed in that place forever, but soon the angels changed formation and disappeared into the heavens, carrying with them the vision of Jesus.

I was so overwhelmed by what I had seen that all I could do was sit down on the floor and wonder whether I had been dreaming or my vivid imagination had been working overtime. After a few moments I noticed that a close friend was sitting on the floor next to me staring into space. "I can't believe what I just saw!" she blurted out. "I saw thousands and thousands of angels and Jesus sitting on a throne."

There are no words to express what I felt at that moment—it was somewhere between shock and disbelief. I will never know how or why the Lord allowed both of us to see the same vision at the same time. It was clear that God was trying to show me something, but I couldn't figure out what.

The answer came the next morning as I was preparing to leave Lake Arrowhead. I was taking one last walk across the grounds and for the first time as a new Christian I felt I heard the voice of the Lord speaking as clearly as someone walking next to me.

I know that sounds strange. I don't want you to get the idea that I'm somehow more spiritual than anyone else. Maybe I didn't hear Him with my ears—but I know I heard Him with my heart.

This is what I felt He was saying to me: *Before last night, you only saw Me as a prophet that walked the earth performing miracles and saving the lost. But I want you to know without a shadow of a doubt that I am more than a man. I am Jesus, the Son of God, the ruler of heaven and earth. I don't want you to be afraid of Satan or the attacks of people, for I am with you and all power is in My hand.*

The vision had revealed the true identity and power of Christ in my life. It has stayed with me until this very day. It has given me an unshakable faith that "greater is He who is in me than he who is in the world." From that time forward, at certain important junctures in my life the Lord has seen fit to allow me visions of His plan for my life.

The Lord also gives us clear vision and direction as we gain a greater understanding of His Word and begin applying it to our lives. If you desire to become a mature Christian with a clear vision of God's will for your life, it is imperative that you find a church where you can submit yourself to a pastor who preaches and teaches the Word of God.

I often talk to women who are frustrated because they don't have a clear direction for their lives. It has been my experience that many times God will not reveal His will until we become spiritually stable and mature. As you bask in strong leadership and grow in your faith, I can almost promise that you will soon begin to perceive the direction God has for your life.

THE VALUE OF VISIONS

Whether or not you receive special revelations from God in visual images doesn't matter. What matters is that you seek God's guidance—and that when you receive it, you follow it.

In order for you to make full use of the gift of God's vision for your life, you should be aware of the following principles.

A Vision Is Always Greater than Your Natural Ability

Sometimes God reveals His divine plan in full-blown technicolor vision. I can only imagine how Moses must have felt when God said, "Tell Pharaoh to let My people go."

Moses tried to persuade God that what He was proposing was at best a flawed idea. "Why should Pharaoh listen to me? Besides, I don't even know how to prepare a speech!"

Naturally, the Lord was not pleased with this resistance from His soon-to-be champion. It took time for such a big vision to sink in to Moses' limited mind.

Not only did the Lord show Moses a colossal vision, He also meant it to be shared with the millions of Jewish people who were living in slavery. The Lord works through leaders to give people direction for their lives.

Much as He did with Moses, the Lord will often extend a call to the very people who couldn't imagine themselves leading other people. I can still remember one year when I attended the Congressional Prayer Breakfast in Washington, D.C. At one of the events they were honoring a woman for her work with the homeless.

Her story had begun ten years prior when she had become homeless with two young children. Winter was about to set in and for days and weeks she begged God to provide a place for her to stay. One day she came across an abandoned school building; out of desperation, she moved into the building with her children.

To her amazement she discovered that the electricity and the water were still on, so she fixed up an empty classroom and made a home for her family. In the days that followed she encountered a homeless man with carpentry skills. The man also moved into the building and with the help of more friends began to repair the deserted classrooms. Soon the building was filled with homeless families, all of which were in need of shelter from the cold. Over a ten-year period, this same woman and a team of volunteers renovated abandoned houses and buildings all over the city.

How could she have known from her meager start that God had a wonderful vision for her life? He revealed it to her one step at a time. Over the years she has been celebrated as a champion of the homeless, helping hundreds and then thousands of people find homes.

Even with a renewed mind, it is sometimes hard to grasp the awesome plan that God has for your life. Through Isaiah, the Lord has given us a glimpse of how we should view His divine nature:

"For My thoughts are not your thoughts,
  Nor are your ways My ways," says the LORD.
"For as the heavens are higher than the earth,
  So are My ways higher than your ways,
And My thoughts than your thoughts." (Isaiah 55:8–9)

Please understand that if God's plan for your life was something you could think up all by yourself, there would be no need for Him to guide you. When the Lord reveals something to you that is bigger than what you can handle, you may rest assured that He has already gone ahead of you to make the impossible possible. When God gives a vision, He also gives *provision*.

The Lord Will Always Confirm His Vision

A vision from God can bring joy, laughter, even disbelief—but it can also bring fear and resistance. However, when the vision of the Lord reaches the fullness of time, rest assured that God is faithful and will bring it to pass.

I can almost hear you thinking to yourself, *But how will I know if what I am seeing or hearing is really from God?* I'm so glad you asked! You see, if the vision is truly from God, it will manifest itself at God's appointed time and you will be given confirmations along the way.

The prophet Habakkuk had a similar question. Listen to how the Lord responded to him:

Write the vision
> And make it plain on tablets,
That he may run who reads it.
> For the vision is yet for an appointed time;
But at the end it will speak, and it will not lie.
> Though it tarries, wait for it;
Because it will surely come,
> It will not tarry. (Habakkuk 2:2–3)

In the same way, when the Lord shows you something that seems difficult or even impossible in the natural realm, write the vision down and keep it in your heart as you wait for it to come to pass. If the Lord has given you a vision that requires action, take one step at a time and wait for the Lord to confirm His words by making a way for you to continue.

Let me caution you to wait for the leading of the Holy Spirit before you reveal your vision to others. When your direction comes from a supernatural source, you may find that those who have no spiritual discernment do not understand or support your vision. Continue to pray for the guidance of the Lord; He is capable of working supernaturally in your life.

I remember the first time the Lord revealed to me in a vision that I was going to write a book. I had a mental image that would not go away. I kept seeing myself sitting at a table autographing books. I remember telling the Lord that I couldn't write a book because I didn't even have a good computer.

Soon after that I spoke at a church. A young woman approached me after the service and placed a check in my hand for three thousand dollars. There was a note with the check that said, "The Lord told me you needed this money." I had never shared my vision with anyone, but the gift from the young woman was a clear confirmation. I purchased a computer and sure enough, a year later I was sitting at a table signing books. The vision came to pass.

A Vision May Require Action

When God shows you a vision and then confirms that vision with signs you cannot ignore, it will stir your faith. When the prophet Habakkuk saw a vision of what the Lord was about to do, he could not imagine how the Lord could possibly work things out. The answer that the Lord gave Habakkuk settled the prophet's doubts and fears. But it also became one of the foundational Scriptures of our faith: "The just shall live by his faith" (Habakkuk 2:4).

The woman in our story must have felt the same way when she was directed to confront the men who had brought the diseased cows into her village. In order to face the challenge that was set before her, she had to release her fears into the hands of God and become totally reliant on His power to protect her and to crush the plans of the wicked herdsmen.

That's what faith does: It takes you into a place where you feel defenseless and vulnerable, yet are fully protected by the power and grace of God. If God doesn't come through, you think, you're going to be in big trouble—but of course He always does.

I like to imagine faith as a long rope. One end of the rope is wrapped around the vision, located in the heavenly realm. The other end of the rope dangles in front of you. No one else can see it. Your assignment is to pull the "faith" rope as hard as you can, until the vision is brought down from the invisible heavenly realm into the visible earthly realm. Pulling on the invisible rope simply means you must perform the work God requires because you believe the vision will come true.

Noah had a vision of rain covering the earth. By faith he was required to build a boat and gather the animals together. Without a clear vision from the Lord, I am certain that Noah would not have undertaken such a massive project. But when the rope of faith dangled from heaven, Noah refused to let go. He worked hard until the ark was completed and the animals were on board. And just as the Lord promised, it rained. "The just shall live by their faith."

Disobedience Can Alter or Abort a Vision

A young woman in my Bible study asked me a very challenging question: "How will I know if God wants me to stop what I'm doing and follow what I think is a new vision?" I certainly know what it feels like to be pulled in several directions at one time and become confused about the Lord's direction. Over the years I have learned there is a time and a season for the visions God reveals to me. Just because He shows you something doesn't always mean that you have to jump up at that very moment and pursue the vision.

Habakkuk reminds us that "the vision is yet for an appointed time." I believe that God is a God of order and that He delights in the completion of the task He has set before us. I spent years as a full-time mom, but as soon as my youngest daughter graduated from high school the Lord called me into full-time ministry. While my daughters were very young I had one vision and one vision alone: I was committed to helping them achieve the things God had shown me for their lives.

Many attractive opportunities came along, but I had to keep my eye on the vision for that season of my life. Sometimes the Lord would show me visions of a time when I would enter into the ministry, but I could also see that it was for an appointed time.

If the enemy can get you to spread yourself thin, then Satan can succeed in disrupting God's vision for your life. Be careful that you don't allow Satan to wear you down with exhaustion by inspiring you to chase several visions at the same time—all in the name of the Lord. Pray for wisdom so that you don't miss the perfect timing of God's vision for your life.

It is sad but true that disobedience can alter or even abort a vision. God called Moses to be the leader who would bring the children of Israel into the Promised Land, but because of disobedience he and most of the people who left captivity behind in Egypt never saw the fulfillment of the vision.

When the children of Israel complained about being thirsty and having no water to drink, the Lord came to Moses in a vision and told him to speak to the rock and that water would flow out. Moses was angry with the people because of their murmuring. So, instead of following God's orders, he struck the rock with his staff. In doing so, he incurred the wrath of God. This is what the Lord said:

> Surely not one of these men of this evil generation shall see that good land of which I swore to give to your fathers, except Caleb the son of Jephunneh; he shall see it, and to him and his children I am giving the land on which he walked, because he wholly followed the LORD. (Deuteronomy 1:35–36)

Because you have a free will, you can reject the vision that God has for your life. But if you choose to accept the vision, then somewhere along the way you decide to do your own thing, God just might give you a pink slip and find a new and obedient servant, like Joshua, who will remain faithful to the vision.

Satan Seeks to Destroy the Manifestation of God's Vision

When King Herod heard from the wise men that the King of the Jews had been born somewhere in his kingdom, he was inspired by Satan to search for the baby Jesus to kill Him. But God did not bring Jesus to earth to be murdered by a jealous king. In a vision, Joseph saw an angel who revealed that Jesus would save His people from their sins. In another vision, the wise men were warned to depart to their home country. They were told not to return to King Herod, who would have tried to learn where Jesus was so as to kill Him.

In order to overcome the plots of Satan, it is important that you wait for God's directions and then act in complete obedience to His will. All the time Jesus was on earth, Satan plotted to destroy the vision that God the Father had for His Son. Even while Jesus was still a baby, God sent visions and dreams to protect His life:

> Now when they had departed, behold, an angel of the Lord appeared to Joseph in a dream, saying, "Arise, take the young Child and His mother, flee to Egypt, and stay there until I bring you word; for Herod will seek the young Child to destroy Him." (Matthew 2:13)

Many times the leading of the Lord may not have anything to do with you directly. You may simply be an instrument that the Lord is using at that moment. In the ninth chapter of Acts, a man named Ananias was directed by a vision from the Lord to go to Straight Street and find a man called Saul of Tarsus. At first Ananias resisted; he knew of Saul's reputation for persecuting Christians. But once the Lord revealed to Ananias that Saul had been chosen by God to become one of the leaders of the church, Ananias obeyed the vision of the Lord.

The people around you may not understand why you have so much courage and hope in the face of adversity. But once the Lord gives you a clear vision of how He will protect you from the attack of the enemy, your faith—which is literally a belief in something despite the absence of tangible proof—will help you face the most difficult challenge because you already know the outcome.

No matter where I am going or what I am doing, I try not to be distracted by the circumstances around me. I make sure to keep my spirit open to the leading of the Lord. Obedience and vision walk hand in hand.

THE IMMEASURABLE IMPACT OF A FULFILLED VISION

The woman in our story who was led to save her people from the diseased cattle probably accomplished much more than she realized. Perhaps a future leader, scientist, or inventor was among the children who would have been poisoned if she had not been led to intervene. That is why you can't allow yourself to be discouraged when the people around you have difficulty understanding what God is showing you. In the case of the woman in our story, the elders eventually understood that God was using her to implement His perfect will.

Remember that for every one of Satan's plans, God has a counterplan. That's exactly what the Cross represents. Through the death and resurrection of Jesus, God redeemed us from Satan's plan to destroy our souls. The same thing happened to the women in our story. When she became fearful that her actions against the evil herdsmen would fail, the Lord had to remind her that it was not her plan but His. And God never fails.

Even when it appears that the vision God has shown you will never come to pass, from time to time there will be a sign or a word from a stranger confirming it. The Lord reminded Habakkuk that though the vision tarries, wait for it; because it will surely come to pass. Maybe at this moment you think that something you are hoping for will never happen. There's one word I want you to remember: suddenly.

I love the word *suddenly*, because so often when God brings a vision to pass He does it *suddenly*. When we are tired of waiting or on the brink of collapse, the Lord will send confirmations to keep us holding on to the vision. Then, when we least expect it, the vision will suddenly be fulfilled.

Expect God to bring the vision to pass. Embrace the visionary role that only a woman can fulfill.

CHAPTER THIRTEEN

Continuing to Live

The woman in our story finally came to a place where she found honor, rest, and love. After having endured the furnace of affliction, she was able to rejoice in the blessings of the Lord without the residue of pride or bitterness. She resisted God's plan at first, like so many of us do, but with the unfolding of each new phase of her life she discovered that His plan was perfect. Like the woman in our story, you must first pass through many seasons of preparation.

When I think about your time of preparation, I picture a dressmaker unfolding a bolt of beautiful and expensive fabric. Now I want you to put yourself into the "mind" of the fabric. Think of how proud the fabric must feel to be so finely woven, sparkling with threads of gold and splashes of color. The dressmaker runs her hand across the smooth fabric as she thinks of the wonderful design that is in her mind. She lifts the scissors from the table and—to the horror of the fabric—begins to make sweeping cuts. The fabric is shocked and humiliated to see portions of itself being tossed into the trash. Why does the dressmaker do it? Because those portions cannot be used in her design. It isn't until the dressmaker has completed her work that the fabric finally understands the process of cutting, throwing away certain parts, then fitting together the pieces that will transform the cloth into a garment that is not only beautiful but useful.

The woman in our story also went through a season of painful preparation, but when the Lord had finished His work she was perfect for His purpose—beautiful and complete, both inside and out. The analogy of the fabric illustrates the frustration you may feel when you don't understand why the Lord is making dramatic changes in your life.

With each new transition, the Lord nudges you on to a new adventure that He has prepared for you. I sometimes picture God as a mother bird placing sharp objects into a nest that was once comfortable and secure. The sharp objects are not designed to hurt the young birds, but to force them to spread their wings and fly. Life is a journey. Even when you find a comfortable nesting place, the Lord will always be there to remind you that your final resting place is not in this world. Until you reach your heavenly destination, you must continue to pursue God's plan for your life.

Many years ago, my sister allowed her son, Todd, to spend part of the Christmas holiday with our family in California. We were so excited about Todd's visit that we went shopping and purchased a number of his favorite toys. My sister put Todd on a nonstop flight to California and entrusted him to the flight attendant who was also responsible for several other children that were flying solo across the country. Somewhere over Washington, D.C., there was a bad storm and the plane was forced to make an unscheduled landing.

Beneath the watchful eye of the flight attendants, Todd and the other children were taken to a hotel suite where they were given all the hamburgers, sodas, and ice cream they could consume.

As soon as the children were settled in for the evening, the flight attendant called to let me know that Todd would not be arriving until the next day. Todd came to the telephone, full of excitement. "Do I have to come to California for Christmas? Why can't I just stay here with the kids from the airplane?"

There are times in life when we are having such a great time that we don't want to move on. How could Todd know that under a Christmas tree in California there where stacks of presents purchased just for him? Much like my nephew, we sometimes can't imagine anything being better than "the kids from the airplane." But as we continue to live, we discover that God has a perfect plan to make our lives rich and full from beginning to end.

GOING THE DISTANCE

When you were very young, you may have wondered, *What could be more wonderful than a trip to Disneyland?* As you aged, new things sounded exciting. What could be more wonderful than going to your high school prom with the boy of your dreams? What could be more exciting than going away to college and being on your own for the first time in your life? Surely nothing could be more fabulous than getting engaged and having a storybook wedding. How about moving into your dream house, or having your first baby? But what can top holding your first grandchild, or celebrating your fiftieth wedding anniversary?

Let me add one more to the list. What could be better than living to see your children saved and serving God?

More and more I encounter women who are suffering from mild cases of arrested development. If their high school years were better than their married lives, they begin to regress and act like teenagers instead of mature wives and mothers.

Other women may hate the idea of aging, so they run to plastic surgeons or buy clothes designed for the MTV crowd. You've probably seen one of these women in the supermarket or at church looking more like a little girl who was caught playing in her mother's makeup than a sober, godly woman entering the best years of her life. The apostle Paul wrote this beautiful reminder to the

Corinthians: "When I was a child, I spoke and thought and reasoned as a child does. But when I grew up, I put away childish things" (1 Corinthians 13:11, NLT).

I hope you will take the time to assess the level of your overall maturity. Ask yourself if you are really growing up or if you are instead stuck in the past because you don't want to face the present or are not prepared to continue into the future.

Perhaps you are afraid about what the future holds. If so, take this Scripture to heart like a warm cup of tea: "For I know the thoughts that I think toward you, says the LORD, thoughts of peace and not of evil, to give you a future and a hope" (Jeremiah 29:11).

God has a plan for you that's good to the very last drop. But it only unfolds as you *continue to live.* God designed life to take you from mountaintop to mountaintop. Sounds good, right? Of course, you realize that to do that you'll have to pass through the valleys in between. But once you taste the sweetness of mountaintop living, you'll find the bitter moments in the valley more bearable.

My earnest hope is that you won't allow yourself to become frustrated by the inevitability of the passing of time and the changes that it brings. Some women think if they haven't achieved certain things by thirty then they've missed the boat. At forty they're over the hill. At fifty they should start making funeral arrangements. At sixty and older, they're practically the walking dead. (I hope you're laughing with me.) If you were to look back over the stages of your life, you would find good and bad in every one.

A young woman experiences delight at moving into her first apartment or decorating her first new home. An older woman rejoices when her children leave home and she has time for other things.

A younger woman talks your ear off about her trip to Italy with her girlfriends or delights in sending you a Christmas card with the first photo of her husband and children. An older woman throws a party because she no longer has to carpool her kids to school, music

ly weapon or unlimited wealth—so the Lord uses the tools of
ission and humbling to prepare His children for the serious
onsibility of being exalted.

f you are crying out to be lifted out of obscurity into promi-
e, then be prepared to submit yourself to a process that is very
bling. Even if you are not seeking to be exalted, the humbling
riences that you are going through could very well mean that
is planning to lift you up and show you off as a demonstration
is grace and glory.

ifice and Obedience

second spiritual team that will bring you closer to the blessings
has in store for you are *sacrifice* and *obedience*. There are two
s of sacrifice that can be offered to the Lord. One is the sacrifice
ossessions and the other is the sacrifice of an obedient and pli-
spirit. The Lord views a sacrifice of possessions with delight and
ptance when you are walking in obedience before Him:
old, to obey is better than sacrifice" (1 Samuel 15:22b).

Sacrifice of your time, talents, and resources are ways of giving
ks to God and acknowledging Him as the source of all that you
sess. If you take out your checkbook and daily planner and note
v you spend your money and time, you will have a strong indi-
on of your true relationship with God. If you place all your sac-
es on the altar of your job or activities that have nothing to do
h God, the things that rule your heart are not godly.

King Solomon shows us another type of sacrifice. When he first
an his reign over Israel, he made a memorial sacrifice of one
usand cows and then asked the Lord to give Him wisdom in
ving the people. The Lord was pleased with Solomon's willing-
s to sacrifice himself in service, so pleased that He bestowed
re wisdom on Solomon than any other king before or since (1
gs 3:7–13). Remember, it wasn't the thousand cows that moved

lessons, sporting events, the dentist, or the mall.

A younger woman lives in a time of adventure and discovery,
including the melodrama of making awful mistakes, yet still has
enough strength to start all over again. An older woman smiles as
she cashes her retirement checks and takes off to see the world.

The most important thing to consider in the passage of time is
that you live your life in such a way that on the day you meet the
Lord He says, "Well done."

COMPANIONS FOR THE JOURNEY

The Bible often mentions godly qualities in pairs.[1] In the Twenty-
third Psalm, for example, "goodness and mercy" follow all the days
of our lives. In the eleventh chapter of Isaiah there are references to
the spirit of "wisdom and understanding" resting on the coming
Messiah. In the first chapter of John, it is written that Jesus was full
of "grace and truth."

With each step that you take toward the ever-unfolding plan of
God, try to imagine these coupled truths as escorts, one on each
side, walking beside you.

Submission and Humility

The first two teacher-escorts that will be sent to help you are *submission* and *humility*. In spite of all the Scriptures that clearly speak
of the rewards for people practicing submission and humility, many
of us continue to struggle with the idea of fully submitting ourselves
to the will of God, even while joyfully singing "I Surrender All." It is
unfortunate that so many women don't understand that phrases like
"submit yourself" and "humble yourself" are keys that open doors to
the blessings of the Lord.

To *submit* means to allow the Lord to have full reign and control
in every area of your life. The attitude of a submissive woman is
reflected in her willingness to submit to her husband (if she's mar-

ried), her boss (if she works), her instructors (if she's a student), and her pastor (every woman should have one).

Don't mistake submission for weakness. A submitted woman carefully chooses the people that she allows to bring covering and guidance to her life. Because she is submitted in the most important areas of her life, she is pliable and flows easily with the people around her.

To *humble* yourself means to acknowledge your limitations and inadequacies and your need for God's rulership over the affairs of your life. A woman with a humble spirit is first of all teachable. In a world that is constantly changing, there will always be new things to learn. Humility will allow older women to listen to and even embrace new ideas. Younger women who are humble will listen to and accept the counsel of those that are older and wiser.

Scripture teaches that we are guaranteed to reap blessings when we embrace humility and submission:

> Likewise you younger people, submit yourselves to your elders. Yes, all of you be submissive to one another, and be clothed with humility, for
> > "God resists the proud,
> > But gives grace to the humble."
> Therefore humble yourselves under the mighty hand of God, that He may exalt you in due time. (1 Peter 5:5–6)

Two major blessings arise from a humble, submissive attitude. First, God gives grace to the humble. Nothing is more wonderful than to be adorned with the grace of God. Grace is the catalysis for such a wide range of blessings that I hardly know where to begin.

Let me explain it this way: You may do your best to live a life that is pleasing to God, but you will always fall short. Even when transformation takes place in your life you will only be perfect when

your body takes its last breath and you step into im... then you need the grace of God to protect you from... you deserve and to release the blessings you do not...

Grace is God's unmerited kindness. It cannot be... behavior or good deeds. It is an open display of God... tiality from God in the face of an enemy who deman... the consequences of our mistakes. Because of grace,... our faults and shortcomings and chooses to make u... ries of His many blessings.

All that grace requires is that you humble you... transforming hand of God. Confess to God when you... actions are not godly. Ask forgiveness from those wh... have offended. Never allow the blessings of God to cau... down on others. Continue to remind yourself that all y... you have accomplished is by the grace of God.

Humility unlocks a second promise from God: He... humble in due time. The experiences that the woma... faced were very humbling. How could she know that... experiences were creating stepping stones that were... higher and higher ground? Without the due proces... being exalted only makes you a candidate for disas... time to become stable and mature enough to sit in hi... representative of the Most High God.

Due time spent in the basement of failure helps you... success. If you stay in the prison of rejection for a lo... due time you will outgrow the need for acceptance fr... you are in need with nothing to depend on but the... for your provision, in due time you will enter into a se... perity and your gratitude will belong to God and God...

To be exalted means to be lifted up to a place... honor, and power. Just as a wise parent would not g... child access to things he is not mature enough to ha...

the Lord to bless Solomon, but a sacrifice that reflected the great love that was in his heart.

To obey is like following a treasure map that leads to a great fortune. If you obey the instructions of God to the letter it may take time, discipline, and hard work, but in the end you will find the treasure even if it's buried in a secret place. If you decide to disobey—as in throwing away the map or going in search of your own treasure—then you're probably in for a long, futile journey. Even if you should find something shiny that appears to have value, if it is not found by using the map of obedience, I can guarantee that what you've found is fool's gold—it appears to be the real thing, but when put to the test it becomes obvious that it's a fake.

Like their companions before them, *sacrifice* and *obedience* also bring special blessings from the Lord:

> May He remember all your offerings,
> And accept your burnt sacrifice.
> May He grant you according to your heart's desire,
> And fulfill all your purpose. (Psalm 20:3–4)

> Carefully obey the voice of the LORD your God, to observe with care all these commandments which I command you today. For the LORD your God will bless you just as He promised you; you shall lend to many nations, but you shall not borrow; you shall reign over many nations, but they shall not reign over you. (Deuteronomy 15:5)

When the woman in our opening story surrendered fully to the Lord and presented her body as a living sacrifice, the Lord released His wonderful blessings from heaven. What makes sacrifices even more precious in God's sight is when they are made with no thought of personal gain. Real sacrifice is always the result of real love. It was in the true spirit of sacrifice that "God so loved the world that He gave His only begotten Son." Sacrifice challenges you to rise above your fears, overcome your limitations, and defeat your selfishness. It is the ultimate expression of love and devotion.

Self-sacrifice propels you into a supernatural realm where you rise above the crippling effects of self-interest, self-absorption, self-centeredness, and self-pity. The fact is that when you sacrifice to the Lord, it's not a sacrifice at all. Rather, it is a beautiful exchange, one in which no matter how great your offering, the Lord gives a much greater gift in return for your faithfulness.

To obey is to be blessed. I am certain that all Christians wrestle with obedience at one time or another. I picture obedience as a muscle-bound contender who in the past has wrestled me to the floor and pinned me to the mat in order to persuade me to obey God's will for my life. Now that I realize that obedience is the key to blessing, the wrestling matches are a lot less frequent.

Obedience would love to just sit down with you and help you see that no matter what price you have to pay to do what is right it is an investment that will always yield high dividends. While it can certainly be challenging to obey the Word of God, doing so sets a high standard for the people around you. I am persuaded that the woman who obeys God will begin having less trouble with a rebellious husband, children, or grandchildren.

Remember, rebellion is an attitude that usually hangs out with pride. If rebellion becomes a part of you, it will eventually take up residence in the people around you. If you want an obedient and cooperative spirit to permeate your environment, you must have a heart that is willing to obey God.

The book of Deuteronomy mentions one blessing that I pray you will strive to obtain and cherish with all your heart: "You shall reign over many nations, but they shall not reign over you" (Deuteronomy 15:6b). A rebellious nation begins with rebellious people. Rebellious people produce rebellious families. Rebellious families produce rebellious schools and communities.

I want you, as a godly woman, to recognize how your personal obedience to God affects not only the people around you; it also affects the entire nation. If our nation is to continue experiencing the blessings of freedom and to retain dominion and authority over the earth, each woman must become a champion of obedience. Just as the woman in our story saved her village because she was obedient to the voice of God, you too can save your village as you obey the Word of God and follow the leading of the Holy Spirit.

Faith and Patience

The Lord will use a third team to usher you into His blessings: *faith* and *patience*. James 1:3 tells us "the testing of your faith produces patience." In order for you to submit and humble yourself, to sacrifice and obey, and to trust in the faithfulness of God, you will need the guardians of *faith* and *patience*.

To have faith is to believe in and hope for that which cannot be seen with the natural eye, that which cannot be proven to exist, and/or that which is impossible to achieve by human effort. In order for your beliefs to become faith, they must first be tested. If you can endure testing without renouncing your beliefs, then you have faith.

Perhaps you recall that Jesus warned Peter that God had granted Satan permission to put him to the test (Luke 22:31–32). Jesus told Peter that He had prayed Peter's faith would not fail and that when the testing was over Peter would strengthen others. Perseverance under duress is a sign of real faith.

People can tell you over and over how much they love you, but the real measure of love is "faith fullness." Faithfulness means to remain loyal and committed in times of peace or adversity. When you say you have faith, it is measured by your "faith fullness." If you are full of faith, you may stumble like Peter, but in the end you will not abandon what you believe. This is why it is so important for the Lord to produce *patience* in your character. Patience will anchor your faith and allow you to endure times of testing.

Patience can be defined as growth through trials. It is the ability to endure hardships while continuing to wait for the promise. Even when you are laughed at or misunderstood and everyone else has lost hope, your patience never fails.

James points out that patience can only be produced when your faith is put to the test (James 1:3). It is like saying that your body will not become strong without performing strenuous exercises. Faith is like your physical body: The more your body is disciplined through vigorous exercise, the stronger you become. One advertiser uses the slogan "No pain, no gain."

Soldiers do not undergo physical and mental punishment so they can parade around with strong minds and bodies. Soldiers know that in order to win battles they must build patience and endurance because the ability to exercise patience under fire is crucial to survival.

With each new battle that you face you may experience a few bumps and bruises, but as you continue to endure them, your patience muscles will become stronger than ever.

Faith and patience work together to help you inherit God's richest blessings:

> We desire that each one of you show the same diligence to the full assurance of hope until the end, that you do not become sluggish, but imitate those who through faith and patience inherit the promises. (Hebrews 6:11–12)

> For whatever is born of God overcomes the world. And this is the victory that has overcome the world—our faith. (1 John 5:4)

There are two important lessons that can be learned from these powerful verses. First, imitate those who "inherit the promises." Don't you just love women who know how to keep their cool and never lose patience when the heat is on? Have you ever said to such a woman, "I want to be like you when I grow up"? If you are wise and desire to mature in the things of God, I strongly recommend that you find a woman to have as a role model, someone whose godly character is worth imitating.

Few things are worse than a woman who professes to be a mature Christian, but who becomes hysterical and starts making rash decisions the moment the pressure is turned up. I believe that the reason the Lord often turns our lives into classrooms is so that we will learn the important lessons He is trying to teach. The course will not end until the Lord shapes us into women who are calm under fire, patient through adversity, and full of faith that is so deeply anchored in Christ that we never lose our cool.

When trials become your instructors, they reveal your deepest character flaws. Trials also allow you to discover strengths you didn't know you possessed. No one enjoys going through difficult times, but you can rest in the knowledge that even when it seems as though your life has come to a standstill and all hope is gone, God is quietly building your *patience* and will continue to do so until you become "perfect and complete, lacking nothing" (James 1:4).

The second lesson is that faith leads you to victory. When your faith is tested, patience becomes a pillar of strength within you. Then a song will rise in your heart. Let's take a moment to remember the great songs of victorious women that have echoed down through the ages.

And Miriam answered them:
"Sing to the LORD,
For He has triumphed gloriously!

The horse and its rider
He has thrown into the sea!" (Exodus 15:21)

Awake, awake, Deborah!
Awake, awake, sing a song!
Arise, Barak, and lead your captives away,
O son of Abinoam! (Judges 5:12)

And Hannah prayed and said:
"My heart rejoices in the LORD;
My horn is exalted in the LORD.
I smile at my enemies,
Because I rejoice in Your salvation." (1 Samuel 2:1)

All of these great women of faith faced great periods of testing before they were able to share their testimonial songs. Where there is no test, there is no song of victory. Trust me when I say that if the Lord is still forging patience in your spirit, the day *will* come when you will be thankful for the trying of your faith.

You will look back on a time when you felt powerless to stop the enemy's attack upon the people you love. In your mind, you were like a helpless little kitten, afraid of its own shadow. The deceiver did everything in his power to keep you from discovering what the Lord always knew: Your heart was like that of a lioness cub—maturing more and more each day. Once you cut your teeth on the promises of God, the devil's days of influence in your life were numbered. What a joyful discovery when you finally realized that "He who is in you is greater than he who is in the world" (1 John 4:4b).

Don't run from the pain that you sometimes experience— embrace it! Remember that where there is pain, there is gain. Cry if you have to. Get through a bad day, a bad week, or a bad month, but never give up. Continue to live and to embrace God's wondrous plan for you, because the promises of God are nearer than you think.

CHAPTER FOURTEEN

Continuing to Love

The woman in our story loved her husband, and she lost him. She had the love of her son, but a child is not capable of satisfying the deep desire that every woman has for communication, intimacy, friendship, and fellowship. She could have decided that she would never again open her heart to the possibility of losing someone for whom she cared so deeply. But finally she came to understand that finding love is worth a risk, because the gift of love brings life's best fulfillment.

More and more often I encounter people who are seeking love but aren't lovable. I don't mean that they don't know how to give and receive affection; I mean they are not able to love because they don't understand how love works. The world is currently inhabited by many people who did not grow up in an atmosphere where they saw examples of real love—they were never taught how to give and receive love.

Even if you read 1 Corinthians 13, which spells out in great detail what true love is, it may not be enough. You may understand the theory but without role models you still might not understand how to put love into action. It's like a civilian reading directions on how to launch a missile. If you've never done it before and you haven't been around people who know how missiles work, there's a pretty good chance you're going to blow yourself up.

Yet it is all too clear that without love the human race would be doomed. Love is why we care for each other. Without love healthy people would experience mental and emotional collapse. Babies could not survive without the care love affords. The sick, weak, and elderly would be quickly eradicated.

It is critical that above all else each of us learns how to love in the way that God intended for us to love. Even if we make mistakes, we must commit in our heart to continue to love. Take it from me: You cannot continue to live unless you continue to love. Without an expression of love at some level in your life you will wither away.

HUMAN LOVE VS. GOD'S LOVE

There are two types of love that I want to explore with you: horizontal and vertical.

Horizontal Love

Horizontal love flows from one human heart to another. It draws its strength from the emotions. It has conditions that must be met in order for the flow of love to continue. It can be wonderful, exciting, even satisfying—but there is always the chance that human love will dry up or require more devotion than one of the parties is able to supply. The book of Matthew talks about what the world will be like without the presence of God's love:

> And then many will be offended, will betray one another, and will hate one another. Then many false prophets will rise up and deceive many. And because lawlessness will abound, the love of many will grow cold. (Matthew 24:10–12)

Please take note of the reference to "false prophets." When many people think of false prophets, they think of phony religious leaders.

But there are other false prophets in the world who shape our moral and spiritual views of love. The media, entertainers, talk shows hosts, and authors are all vehicles that bring us false messages about love.

I can tell whether a woman has been reading New Age books or talking to television psychics just by engaging in simple conversation with her. Once someone has embraced a false doctrine, she is a sitting target for the pain and confusion that always accompany it.

You would probably agree with me that much of what people call "love" in this day and age is nothing more than unbridled lust, confusion, and perversion. Teenagers fall in and out of what they call love on a regular basis and are left with such aftereffects as disease, unwanted children, abortions, disappointment, and disillusionment—all in the name of love. Adults contribute to the soaring divorce rate and have multiple remarriages that end in multiple divorces—all in the name of love.

Of course there are much darker pursuits in our society, pursuits that some people call love. But I am not led to mention what they are. If you are curious, turn on a talk show for five minutes and you'll get the picture. On second thought, don't.

We have probably all known women who have bought into the philosophy of "love yourself first." This is what many women have come to believe:

- Look out for number one
- Don't let family and friends stand in your way
- Don't worry about love—your career goals should always come first
- Look for a man who has more than you do—don't settle for less
- Don't allow your husband and family to be the center of your life—you must learn how to define your life apart from your family

- Don't allow becoming a mother to control your life—there's always daycare
- Even though you have young children, you can't afford not to work full-time—you have too many expenses, including your luxury auto and credit card debt
- Get a divorce if your husband isn't in tune with your quest for self-identity
- Marriage can be a trap that will keep you from reaching your full potential as a woman
- Being a housewife and mother is an unfulfilling and anti-quated notion
- Maybe you shouldn't have children—they will take up too much of your life

This kind of philosophical deception robs women of the gift of love and family that God designed for them. Protection, fellowship, and emotional support are all parts of a healthy, God-ordained lifestyle.

A clear example of the failure of horizontal love is found in the story of Peter. He was the disciple that claimed to love Jesus yet denied that he knew Him when the Lord was arrested and crucified. Jesus had a different kind of love for Peter. In spite of Peter's betrayal, the compassionate Savior forgave him and continued to love him. Forgiveness is one of the defining virtues that separates human horizontal love from God's vertical love.

After the Resurrection Jesus had a conversation with Peter that dealt with the real meaning of love:

So when they had eaten breakfast, Jesus said to Simon Peter, "Simon, son of Jonah, do you love Me more than these?" He said to Him, "Yes, Lord; You know that I love You." He said to him, "Feed My lambs." (John 21:15)

Three times in a row Jesus asked Peter the same question: "Do you love me?" Three times Peter answered, "Lord, I love you."

Peter may have really thought he loved Jesus, but his love was horizontal love, rooted in emotion. It was this kind of love that failed when Peter was faced with the possibility of suffering and death. As he had watched the soldiers beat Jesus, spit in His face, and mock Him, the fear of dying had overruled the horizontal love that had once stirred Peter's heart.

After the resurrection, Jesus helped Peter to learn the real meaning of love. First, He forgave Peter and restored him to fellowship. Secondly, Jesus demonstrated His confidence in Peter by making him the head of the church.

As Peter confessed his love for Jesus three times, Jesus wasn't listening to the words. He was more focused on the meaning behind the words.

Watch for the Greek words behind the English word "love" in the following exchange. I'll explain more in a minute. For now, just notice that Jesus and Peter are using different words:

"Peter do you love (agape) Me?"

"Yes, Lord, I love (phileo) You."

Jesus was asking Peter about his commitment to love Him. Peter's answer did not speak of commitment, but rather of affection for Jesus.

Agape is the Greek word for God-centered love. This kind of love has nothing to do with feelings.[1] It is love that is expressed through the action it takes. It is unconditional love that expresses commitment regardless of feelings. That's why Jesus was able to forgive Peter and to continue in the relationship even though He had been betrayed by Peter: His love was agape. It is the same word used in the passage that says God so loved (agape) the world that He gave His only Son (John 3:16).

Phileo is a Greek word that refers to an expression of human love.[2] It is based on affectionate feelings and not on the action it takes. Phileo is a love that is based on conditions. As long as the conditions are favorable, phileo is there to support and encourage; but if enough pressure is applied, phileo love will crumble.

Peter was able to phileo love Jesus as much as was humanly possible, but when the terror of Roman punishment became a looming reality, Peter discovered that he did not possess the agape love to maintain his faithfulness.

It is very important that we understand what is really being communicated when we are talking about love. So many couples find themselves in faltering relationships because they misunderstood what was originally being communicated.

A woman may ask, "Do you apple me?" The man replies with a smile, "Honey, I orange you with all my heart." They think they are talking about the same thing, but in reality they're comparing apples and oranges. Her definition of love may mean a three-carat engagement ring and marriage within a year, while he may be saying, "I would love to go over to your place and have wild, passionate sex."

Don't allow yourself to drift into a dream world in which you refuse to deal with the reality of what people really mean when they say, "I love you."

Vertical Love

Vertical love comes from the heart of God. It is an eternal fountain from which the human heart can find an unlimited supply of the strength and compassion it needs to move beyond mere affection to the place where love is demonstrated.

As we can see when Jesus forgave Peter, vertical love is also unconditional. The love that comes from God is for better or for worse. The commitment continues even when "worse" shows up and refuses to go away.

Obviously, you need courage to continue to love. You can find this courage only when your heart is linked upward (vertically) with the love of God.

It used to be that all telephone calls and Internet data traveled through ground-based phone lines. But as phone and e-mail traffic has increased, much of this load has been shifted to communication satellites. So, without the communication satellites that are orbiting above, you would not be be able to have telephone or e-mail conversations with others.

It is no different with vertical love. You must first be connected to God before you can successfully connect to people. That is why couples with problems in their relationship always start a counseling session by saying, "We just don't communicate anymore." Without a vertical uplink to God, communication on a horizontal level will always break down.

Jesus prayed passionately to the Father that your hearts and minds would be filled with the vertical love that can only come from the heart of God. Speaking to God, He said, "I have made you known to them, and will continue to make you known in order that the love you have for me may be in them and that I myself may be in them" (John 17:26, NIV).

The love the Father has for us was expressed by the action He took. The Father was willing to sacrifice the life of His only Son to demonstrate His love for us (Romans 5:8). The Son had to die in order for us to have the vital spiritual organs that would allow us to experience eternal life.

Can you imagine having the kind of love in your heart that would cause you to sacrifice your own life in order that the lives of the people you love might be saved? Just imagine if husbands, wives, families, and friends were willing to sacrifice for each other's lives. Wounded hearts, divorce, and broken families would be things of the past.

The love that comes from God is designed to merge you into loving relationships where you become of one heart, mind, and soul with others. This kind of vertical love can only become complete when you first become one with the Father and the Son. Then you can become one with others in covenants of friendship, marriage, and family.

Jesus' prayer to the Father was that His sacrifice on Calvary's cross would not only bring the gift of salvation, but would also make us eternally one with the Father and the Son. Jesus also prayed that once this great vertical love was deposited within us, we would have the power to remain one with one another.

Once your heart becomes one with Jesus, you no longer have to be afraid of being hurt or feeling rejected. The love of Jesus in you will give you the strength to endure the difficulties that come with human relationships. No matter what happens, the love from the Father and Son will cause you to always triumph. ·

RECOGNIZING COUNTERFEIT LOVE

First Corinthians 13:1–3 tells us that many wonderful practices can be accomplished without love even though they appear to be motivated by love. You can have faith that moves mountains, you can bestow all your goods to feed the poor, you can give your body to be burned—all without love. You can even do them without God.

But whenever you act apart from God, your acts of kindness and your wonderful deeds are counterfeits for the real thing. They are nothing more than the sound of empty brass clanging in the wind. Worst of all, your good intentions often become the tool that Satan uses to destroy you and deceive others.

Remember how the woman in our story "tripped over the man's good intentions and fell into the pit of need"? When the man came to her house to fix the roof, he came equipped with nothing but good intentions. After the man had completed the work, the woman prepared a meal for him to show her gratitude—and she, too, had good intentions. But as someone once so aptly pointed out, the road that leads to hell is paved with good intentions.

When she began to cry tears of loneliness and frustration, the man had no evil thoughts as he took her in his arms to comfort her; the action that he took came from the goodness of his heart. But if he had been ruled by the love of God, he would have prayed with the woman rather than allowing both of them to fall into sin. And if the woman had been ruled by God's love, she would have experienced the peace that passes all understanding rather than the temptation that can lead to sin.

The enemy will use good works to draw you from God and persuade you that you don't need Him to know real love. The enemy may convince you to call your temporary happiness or your charitable deeds "love." But you can never have real love apart from God, because God is love (1 John 4:8).

If you are filled with the love of God but are still having difficulty understanding how to walk in vertical love (and most of us do), I recommend that you seek out a seasoned couple or a mature single woman who has for years demonstrated faithfulness in love and commitment to God and others. Get close to such people and emulate the godly love they demonstrate through their actions toward and treatment of others. Learn from their example of patience and forgiveness.

I once heard someone say that in order to have a lasting relationship, it takes two givers and two forgivers. You may have to live in the land where the divorce rate soars and disregard for human life is rampant, but when you become one with God, you can stand in the blessed assurance that love His never fails.

WOMEN WHO DEMONSTRATE GOD'S LOVE

The woman in our story was motivated to risk her life and save her village for one reason alone: love. While men seem driven by duty to their family or their country, women are driven by love—even when that love requires them to endure more than they ever thought possible.

Ephesians 5 advises wives to submit to their husbands and husbands to love their wives. Notice that Paul didn't have to tell the wives to love. Why? Because for women, love is as natural as breathing. Men, on the other hand, can get so caught up in duty and responsibility that they forget to love.

The Scriptures also tell us that in the last days lawlessness will cause the love of many to grow cold (Matthew 24:12). As women connected to the love of God, we shine the brightest when human love begins to fail. As the world around us collapses because people have rejected God's love, we can continue to give and receive love because we are drawing strength from the Holy Spirit that resides within us. There is no greater way to lead the lost to Christ than by allowing them to see God's shining love at work in our lives.

That is why Jesus said, "By this all will know that you are My disciples, if you have love for one another" (John 13:35).

In the days to come I am persuaded that God will challenge your comfort zone and cause you to demonstrate the power of His love in a way that only a woman can do. As the flames on logs in a fireplace turn to embers, you can take a poker and turn the logs, thereby fanning the flames. The more you disturb the comfort of the logs, the brighter the flames will burn.

In the coldness of this world, people are desperately searching for a brightly burning fire by which they can warm their souls. I pray that your life will represent a warm and comfortable place where people can experience the love of God in action.

In our cross-gender culture, women are stepping into roles that were once restricted to men and men are stepping into roles that were once restricted to women. But there are still some things that only a woman can do. God has set us apart with special talents and gifts to serve His purposes in ways that are uniquely feminine. It's not that men are incapable of performing the same tasks, it's just that God has graced women to do some things better then men—and vice versa.

As you continue to go about the business of living a life that is pleasing to the Lord, I want to leave you with thoughts about a few of the things that only a woman can do:

- Only a woman is willing to sacrifice her ego for the sake of love
- Only a woman knows how to make a child feel safe in the midst of a crisis
- Only a woman listens with her heart as well as her ears
- Only a woman can turn a house into a home
- Only a woman will choose intuition over logic
- Only a woman can make a big salary or run a prosperous business and still love a good sale
- Only a woman is prepared to meet any emergency with the things she carries in her purse
- Only a woman sees the invisible potential in discarded things and discarded people
- Only a woman can change the face of history by influencing men and training children

Before I close this chapter, I want to leave you with a prayer:

Dear Lord, bless my sister with a full awareness of her God-potential. I pray that every hindrance to her spiritual development would cause her to gain new strength as she presses against the walls of her cocoon. I pray that one day she will whisper, "I believe I can fly!"

As she spreads her beautiful wings and soars toward the vision that You have for her life, I pray that You would protect her from the predators that would seek to consume her beauty and power.

Finally, I pray the words of encouragement to my sister

that is in the caterpillar stage, but who will soon be transformed. Lord, please remind every woman who feels unappreciated that each of us must crawl before we can grow wings and fly. May her days on the ground be well spent as she goes through the seasons of preparation that will allow her to fly higher than she ever imagined and to perform the wondrous works that only a woman can do.

Amen.

The publisher and author would love to hear your comments about this book. *Please contact us at:* www.multnomah.net/onlyawoman

Study Guide

PART I: THE STORY OF A WOMAN

[God] is able to do exceedingly abundantly above all that
we ask or think, according to the power that works in us.
(Ephesians 3:20)

There will be times when life will throw you a curve and you will
be forced to deal with your own survival—perhaps even the survival
of those you love. Looking at the woman in our story, what do you
think your response would have been in a similar situation?

Describe a situation in which you were surprised by your own
response to a crisis.

What discoveries and changes did you make after facing a crisis?

Scripture Giveaway

Find a Scripture that points to God's faithfulness in the midst of crisis. Give the verse to someone in need of encouragement.

CHAPTER 1: THE GATEWAY TO CHANGE

So God created man in His own image; in the image of God He created him; male and female He created them. (Genesis 1:27)

Whenever you are faced with a real crisis, a great inner struggle erupts between what you believe you are and what God has called you to become. A good self-image will help you move toward a solid God-image. But if your self-image has been damaged, it will be reflected in a weak God-image. How has your self-image been affirmed? How has it helped you to develop a strong God-image?

How has your self-image been damaged? How has that hindered the development of your God-image?

Your personality is always reflected in your God-image. Are you busy like Martha, preoccupied like Mary, a fighter like Peter, or something else?

Scripture Giveaway

Find a Scripture that reminds a special friend that she is fearfully, wonderfully formed by God.

CHAPTER 2: WAITING TO BE RESCUED

He delivers and rescues,
> And He works signs and wonders
In heaven and on earth,
> Who has delivered Daniel from the power of the lions.
(Daniel 6:27)

The woman in our story searched all over her village for someone to come to her rescue. She soon learned that she was looking in all the wrong places. Have you ever felt so overwhelmed by a difficult situation that you found yourself fantasizing about being rescued out of it?

When you allow people to rescue you, what are some of the possible consequences?

What are the advantages when God helps you to overcome adversity by stirring up the power within you?

Scripture Giveaway

Find a psalm in which the writer pleads to be rescued by the Lord. Pray the psalm over someone in need.

CHAPTER 3: ACCEPTING THE CHALLENGE

Trust in the LORD with all your heart,
>   And lean not on your own understanding;
In all your ways acknowledge Him,
>   And He shall direct your paths. (Proverbs 3:5–6)

When the woman in our story ventured into the forest, she stepped into an unknown realm where she was forced to become completely God-dependent. List and explain what you learned about the different types of dependent behavior.

What does it mean to be God-dependent?

Do you find yourself moving back and forth between being God-dependence and other types of dependencies? Please explain.

Scripture Giveaway

Jesus speaks of depending on His Father: "Of myself I can do nothing." Using your concordance, find and give a Scripture to someone special to remind him or her to depend on the Heavenly Father.

CHAPTER 4: OVERCOMING THE PITFALLS

He also brought me up out of a horrible pit,
>   Out of the miry clay,
And set my feet upon a rock,
>   And established my steps. (Psalm 40:2)

There are times when you might think that you are standing on solid ground but suddenly discover an unforeseen pitfall. Describe a pitfall experience in your life.

Were you angry with God? Were you angry with yourself? What lessons did you learn?

After reading the chapter on pitfalls, can you identify three steps you could take to avoid falling into them?

Scripture Giveaway

Find a Scripture that will warn a friend to beware of pitfalls, then give it to someone in need of exercising wisdom.

CHAPTER 5: FACING THE ENEMY

A good name is to be chosen rather than great riches,
>   Loving favor rather than silver and gold. (Proverbs 22:1)

Sometimes when I have to face my enemies, I feel like Dorothy in *The Wizard of Oz*. I wish I could click my heels three times and disappear. Based on this chapter, what are the two best weapons a woman can use when facing the enemy?

What are some of the attributes of a gracious woman?

What is favor and how did it help Queen Esther? How can favor help you to achieve your desired goals?

Scripture Giveaway
Find a Scripture that details the benefits of being a gracious woman. Give it to a friend.

CHAPTER 6: PRESENTING YOUR PETITION

And if we know that He hears us, whatever we ask, we
know that we have the petitions that we have asked of Him.
(1 John 5:15)

Just as earthly parents listen attentively as their children express
their needs, so our heavenly Father listens with concern to the petitions of our hearts. How well do you wait on the Lord's answer once
you have made your petition?

If the Lord were to present a petition to you, what do you think
He would ask?

Write a petition to Father God, making known the desires of
your heart.

Scripture Giveaway

Ask someone close to you if he or she has a prayer need. Find an
appropriate Scripture based on the need and share it; then stand
with that person in prayer.

CHAPTER 7: CELEBRATING THE VICTORY

Now thanks be to God who always leads us in triumph in Christ. (2 Corinthians 2:14a)

The joy of holding a long-awaited newborn is something that only a woman can understand. It is very similar when a goal is finally reached. Write down a recent victory that the Lord has given. (There is always one to be found—even if it's the victory of living another day.)

Try to identify any strongholds that may be hindering you from experiencing victory in your life.

Write down a prayer, thanking God in advance for the victory.

Scripture Giveaway

Find a Scripture that speaks of victory and triumph. Give it to someone in need of encouragement.

PART II: THE STORY OF A NEW WOMAN

For I consider that the sufferings of this present time are not worthy to be compared with the glory which shall be revealed in us. (Romans 8:18)

Once you have endured a life-altering experience, you may realize that you have become a completely different person. However, it is sometimes difficult for the people in your life to adjust to the changes. Share an experience that changed you dramatically. It might be when you went away to college, became a mother for the first time, or fell in love with your spouse.

What were your feelings as a result of this change? What personal adjustments did you have to make?

How did people in your life respond to the changes they saw in you?

Scripture Giveaway

In the book of Philippians, find the Scripture that says God will complete the work He started in you. Share it with someone who is in the process of completing a demanding task.

CHAPTER 8: THE PROCESS OF TRANSFORMATION

Do not be conformed to this world, but be transformed by the renewing of your mind, that you may prove what is that good and acceptable and perfect will of God. (Romans 12:2)

Transformation can manifest itself through much turbulence or happen as quietly as the dawning of a new day. However the process takes place, the results are designed to make you a new creation. If you have been transformed, was there a time when you doubted God's power to change you? If so, why?

Are you now—or were you ever—at a place in your life where you wondered whether your circumstances would ever change for the better? Explain.

Based on this chapter, what are the challenges of transformation?

Scripture Giveaway

Encourage someone to forget the things of the past and reach toward the things that are ahead. Find the Scripture in Philippians that describes this.

CHAPTER 9: PUTTING ON THE NEW CREATION

Put on the new man who is renewed in knowledge according to the image of Him who created him. (Colossians 3:10)

Every morning, in order to make yourself presentable to the world,
you don the necessary attire. In the same way, God wants you to put
on the proper spiritual attire so that you will be pleasing in His sight.
What are some of those things that can strengthen your spirit?

List the things in your life that you had to put off because they
were hindering your transformation:

If you had the wings of a butterfly, is there still some aspect of
your old life as a caterpillar that you would miss?

Scripture Giveaway

Sing the chorus from *I Believe You Can Fly* to someone who is in
need of encouragement. Then read Philippians 1:6.

CHAPTER 10: SETUPS THAT LEAD TO SETBACKS

Therefore let [her] who thinks [she] stands take heed lest [she] fall. (1 Corinthians 10:12)

The woman in our story experienced public victory and private defeat. Though she saved her village, the elders and her neighbors rejected her new strength and budding leadership skills. Have you ever experienced rejection or loneliness that left you vulnerable to the setups of the enemy? Please explain.

Share some of the ways that Satan can set you up for a setback.

Based on this chapter, what are some of the reasons why God allows you to experience setbacks?

Scripture Giveaway

If there is someone close to you who you believe is being set up by Satan, commit to pray for that person. If the person recognizes the setup, stand together on the Scripture promise found in Job 5:12.

CHAPTER 11: THE RULES OF CONTENTMENT

Let your conduct be without covetousness; be content with such things as you have. For He Himself has said, "I will never leave you nor forsake you." (Hebrews 13:5)

Just as a home should represent a place where you are able to escape and find contentment in the natural realm, so there should be a place in the spiritual realm where you can retreat and find contentment. What are your "rules" for finding spiritual contentment in your life?

Can you identify the things that rob you of your contentment? Please explain.

Based on this chapter, what rules did you learn regarding how to maintain your contentment?

Scripture Giveaway

Find a Scripture that says, "Be anxious for nothing." Give it to someone that is struggling with anxiety.

CHAPTER 12: FOLLOWING GOD'S VISION FOR YOUR LIFE

Where there is no vision, the people perish. (Proverbs 29:18a, KJV)

The woman in our story had to come to a place of complete obedience in order to see the fulfillment of God's vision for her life. Even though it was difficult, she followed where He led and ultimately experienced the blessings of the Lord. Have you ever obeyed the will of God and in doing so received His blessings? Please explain.

Have you ever experienced what you believe was a vision from God? Please explain.

What are other ways God has guided you into His plan?

Based on this chapter, what steps can you take to ensure that your vision is from God?

Scripture Giveaway

Give a friend the encouraging Scripture concerning God's plan for your life—it is found in Jeremiah 29:11.

CHAPTER 13: CONTINUING TO LIVE

When I was a child, I spoke as a child, I understood as a
child, I thought as a child; but when I became a [woman],
I put away childish things. (1 Corinthians 13:11)

There are times when you will have no desire to move on to the next
phase of life. There will be times when you might find it difficult to
continue to open your heart to love. But God encourages you to
continue, for He knows that He has a perfect plan to make your life
rich and full from the beginning to the end. Have you experienced
a time in your life when you found it difficult to move on?

Based on the chapter, how does the Lord prepare us for His
blessings?

What are some of the blessings you experienced when you continued to live?

Scripture Giveaway

A passage in John begins, "If you continue in My Word…" Look up
the entire Scripture and encourage someone with it.

CHAPTER 14: CONTINUING TO LOVE

Love never fails. (1 Corinthians 13:8a)

Love can come from emotion or it can come from the heart of God. Discovering the difference between the two kinds of love can be quite an experience. Explain how Peter was changed by love.

Describe an experience you've had with horizontal love.

Describe an experience you've had with vertical love.

Scripture Giveaway

Find a person that needs a clear demonstration of love. Give her a card with a Scripture that says, "I love you, from God."

NOTES

Chapter 1

1. Ulmer, Kenneth C., *Spiritually Fit To Run the Race,* (Nashville: Thomas Nelson, Publishing 1999), 168.

Chapter 2

1. Brown-Driver-Briggs, *Hebrew and English Lexicon* (Peabody, Mass.: Hendrickson Publishers, 1999), 740.

2. Kraemer, D'Angelo, *Women and Christian Origins* (Oxford: Oxford University Press, 1999), 44.

3. Webb, Millie L, *Driven Magazine* (MADD Publications, 2000).

4. Italia and Wallner, *Clara Hale: Mother to Those Who Needed One* (Addot Daughers Publishing 1993).

5. Audain, Cynthia, *Florence Nightingale* (Agnes Scott Publishers, 1998).

6. Lindley, Susan Hill, "You have Stept out of your Place," *A History of Women and Religion in America* (Kentucky: Westminster John Knox Press, 1996), 188.

7. Spink, Kathryn, *The Wisdom of Mother Teresa* (Kentucky: Westminster John Knox Press, 1998), 19.

Chapter 4

1. Brueggmann, Walter, "The Costly Loss of Lament," St. Louis, MS (Aricle, Eden Theological Seminary, 1986).

Chapter 5

1. Brown-Driver-Briggs, 373.

Chapter 7

1. Wilson, Ralph F., *The Story of John Newton* (Christian Articles Archives, 1985).

Chapter 8

1. Vine, W.E., *Expository Dictionary of New Testament Words* (New Jersey: Fleming H. Revell Co.), 227.
2. Ibid., 149.

Chapter 9

1. Brown-Driver-Briggs, 968.

Chapter 10

1. Dunn, John L., *The Sibley Guide to Birds* (Audobon Society, 1999).

Chapter 13

1. Hunnard, Hannah, *Hinds' Feet on High Places* (Wheaton, Ill., Tyndale House, 1975), 132.

Chapter 14

1. Vine, 22.
2. Ibid.